DEAR,

WE WOULD LIKE TO EXTEND A WARM WELCOME TO YOU AND EXPRESS OUR SINCEREST THANKS FOR CHOOSING OUR MANDALA COLORING BOOK AS YOUR CREATIVE OUTLET. WE UNDERSTAND THAT COLORING CAN BE A SOOTHING AND THERAPEUTIC ACTIVITY, AND WE ARE THRILLED TO BE A PART OF YOUR JOURNEY TOWARDS INNER PEACE AND RELAXATION.

THANK YOU FOR CHOOSING OUR MANDALA COLORING BOOK, AND WE WISH YOU ALL THE BEST ON YOUR COLORING JOURNEY

IF YOU HAVE A MINUTE TO SPARE, PLEASE RATE AND REVIEW OUR COLORING BOOK.

SINCERELY,

THE AUTHOR

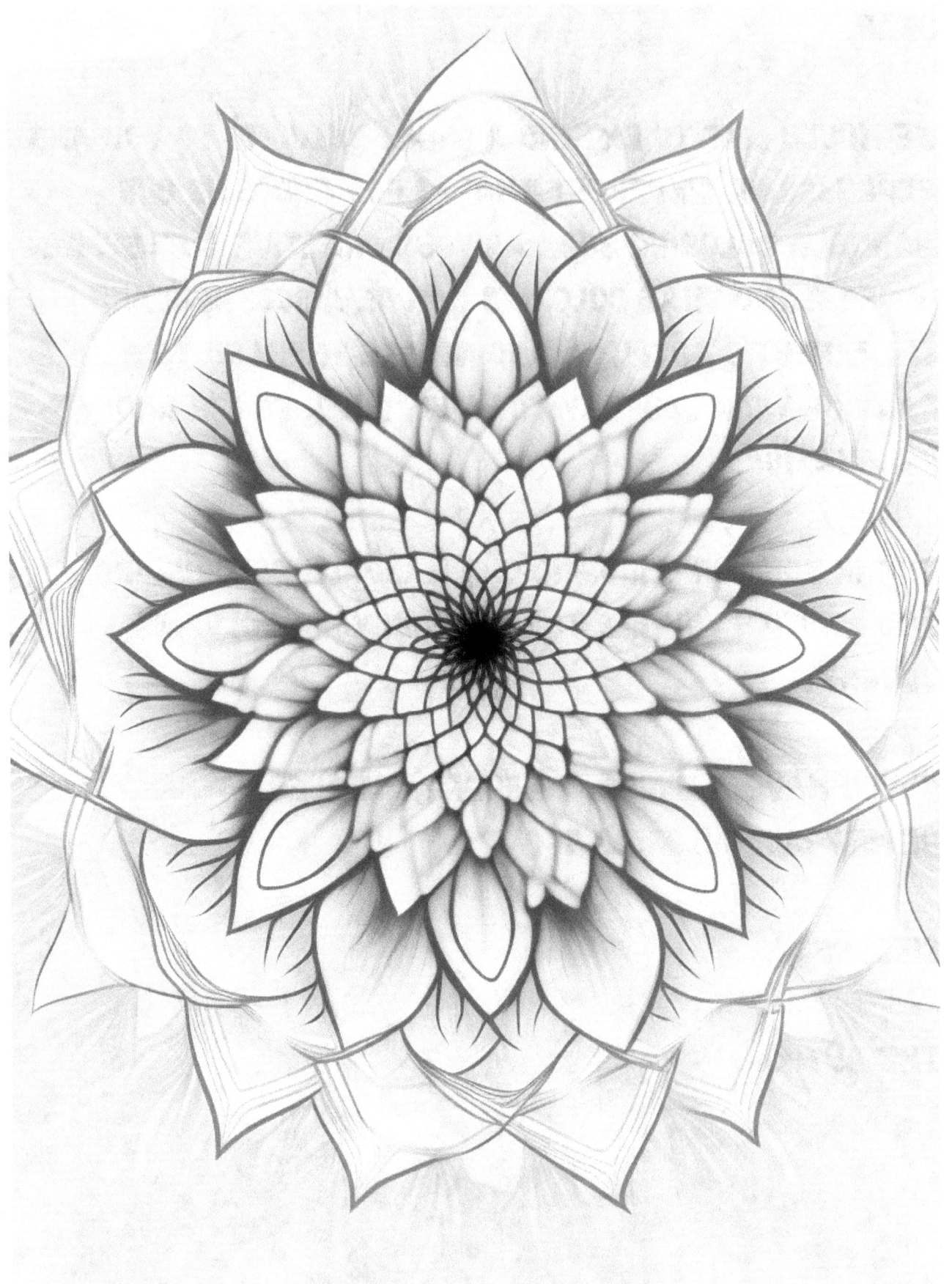

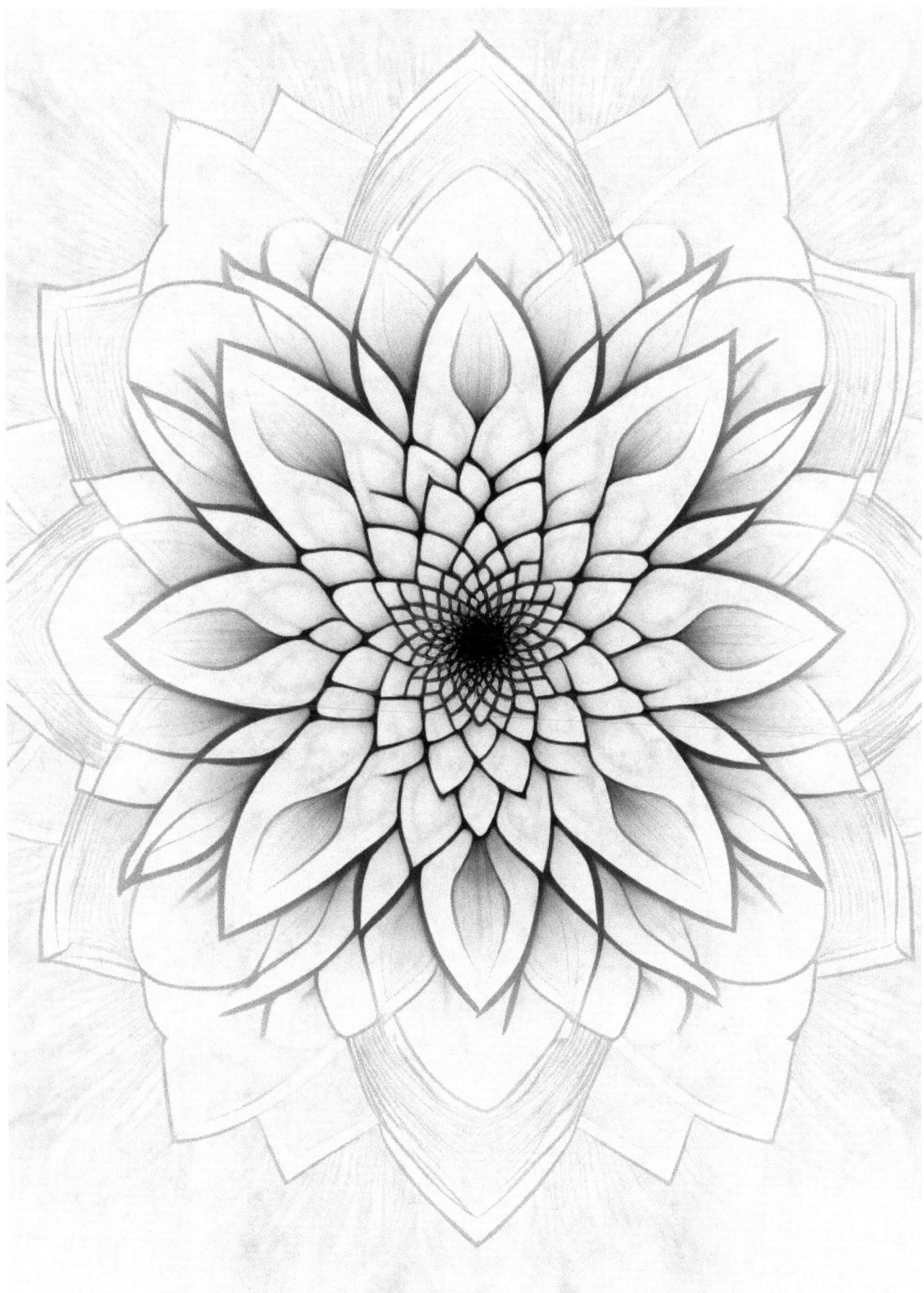

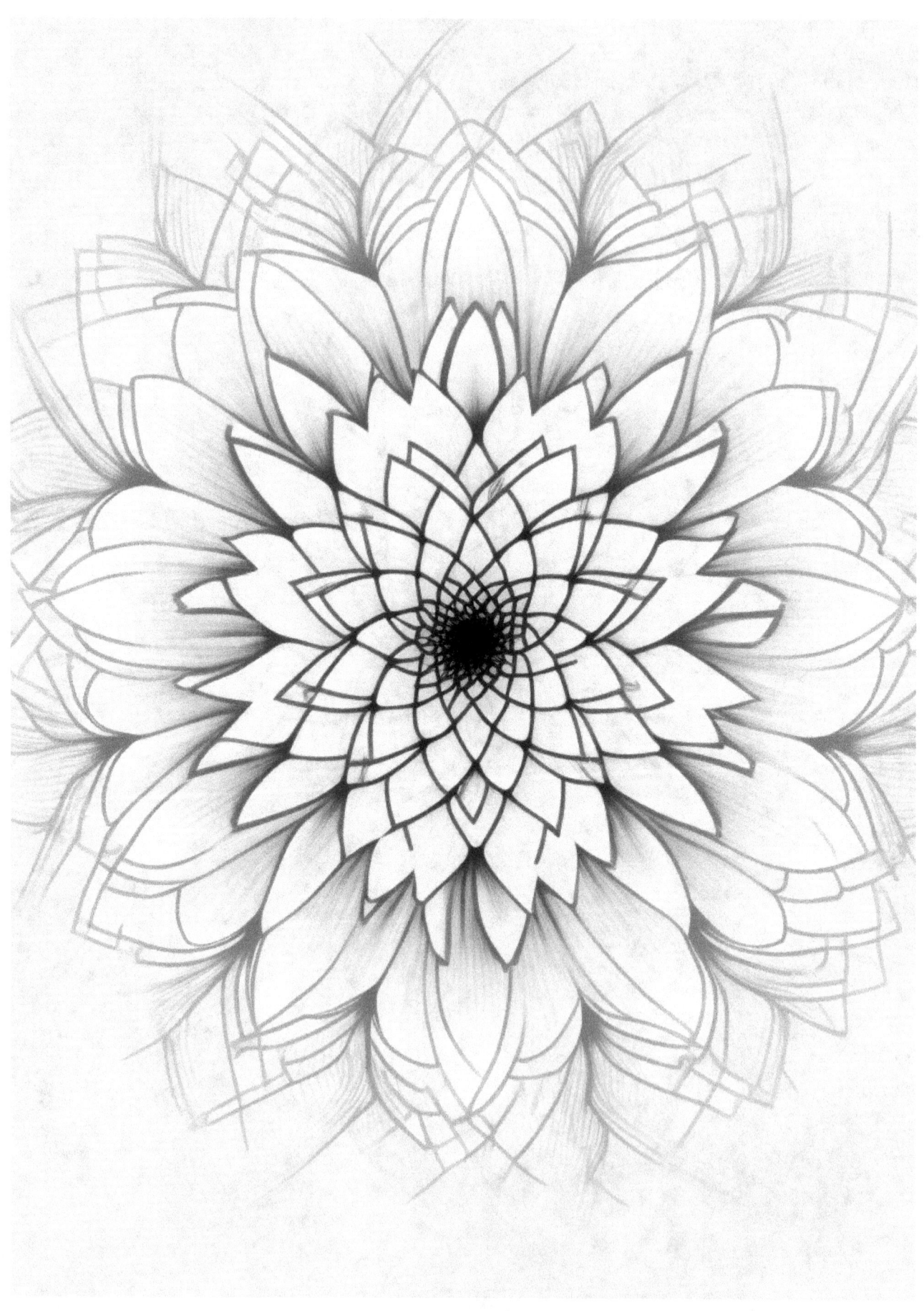

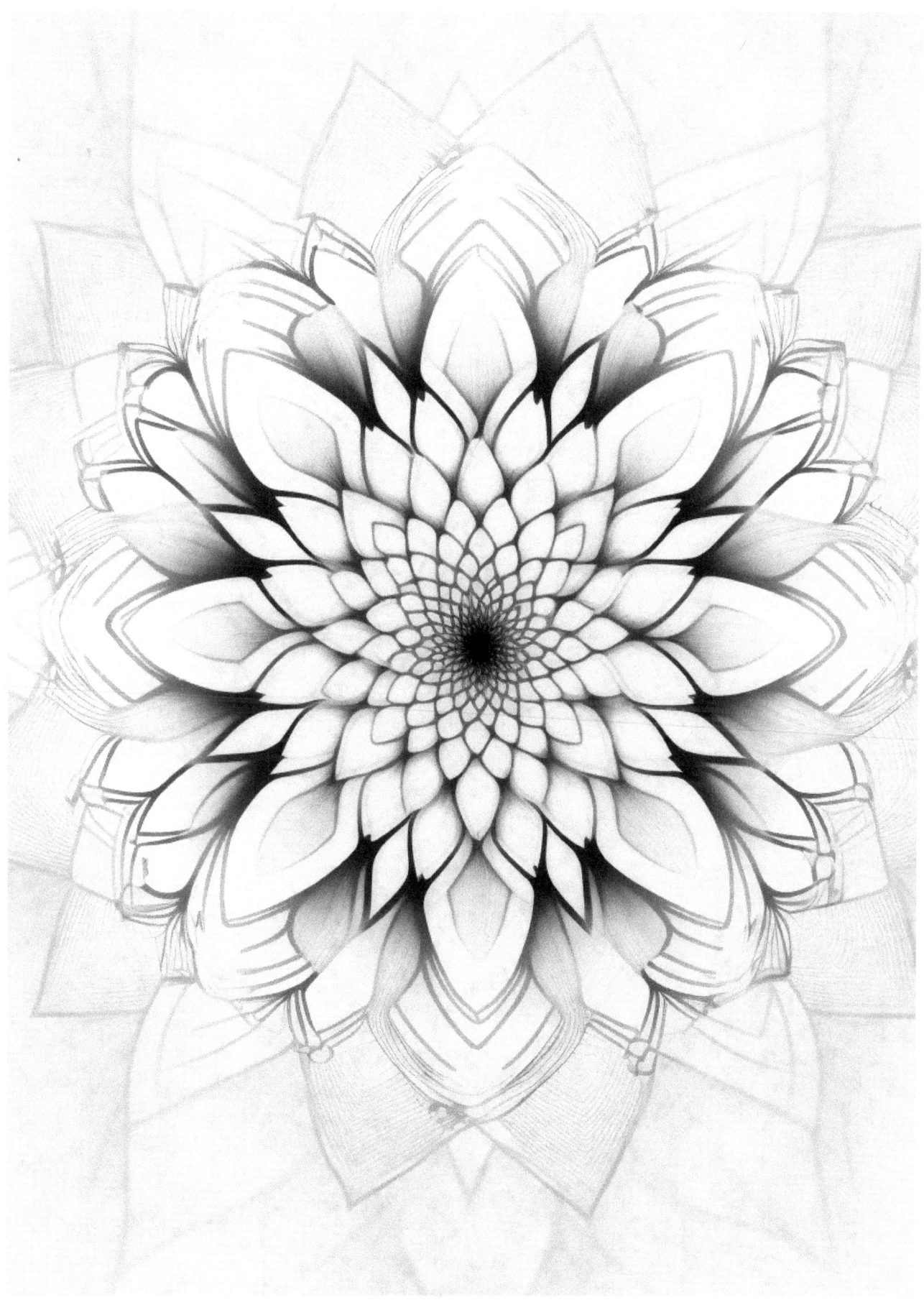

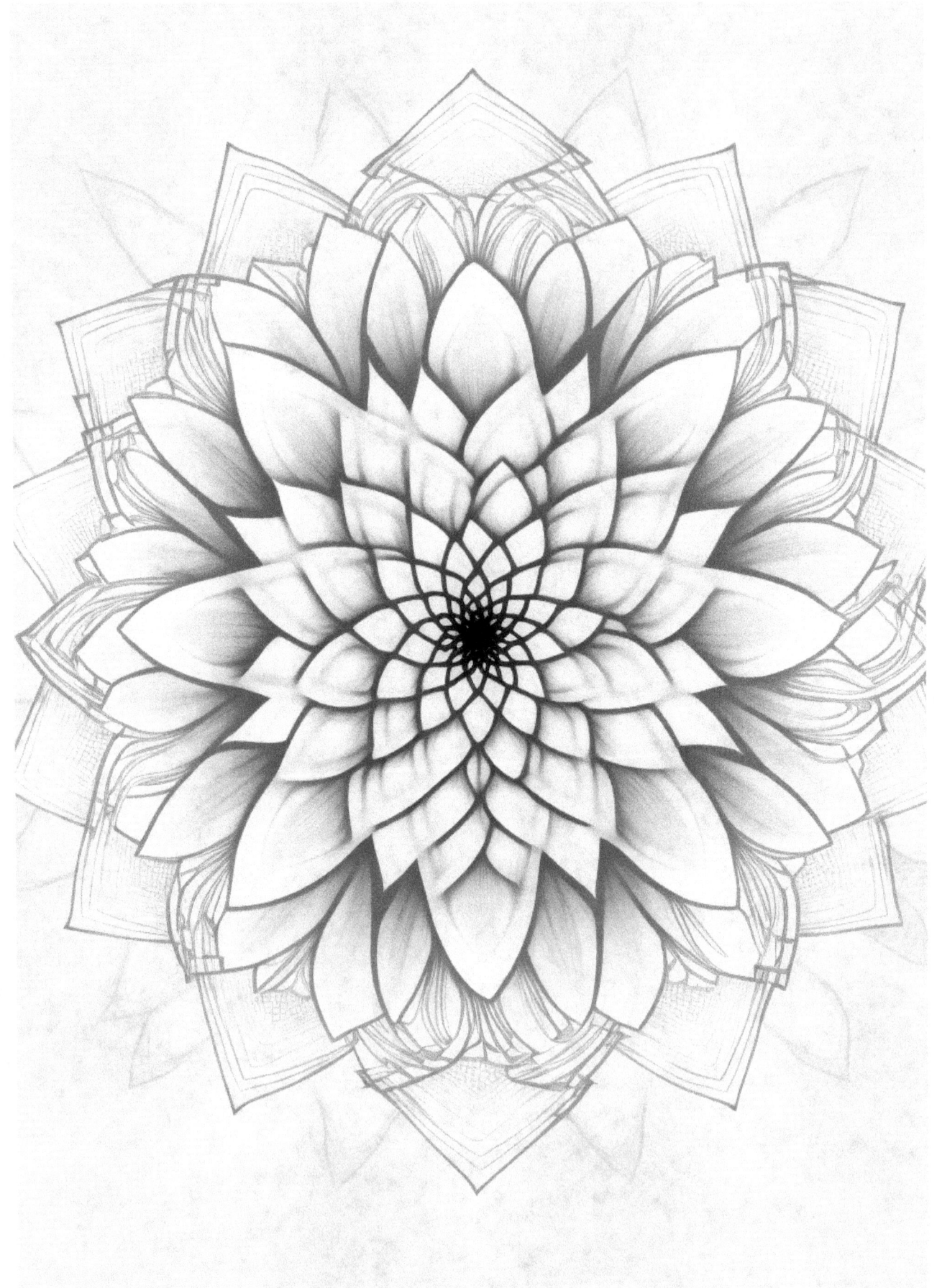

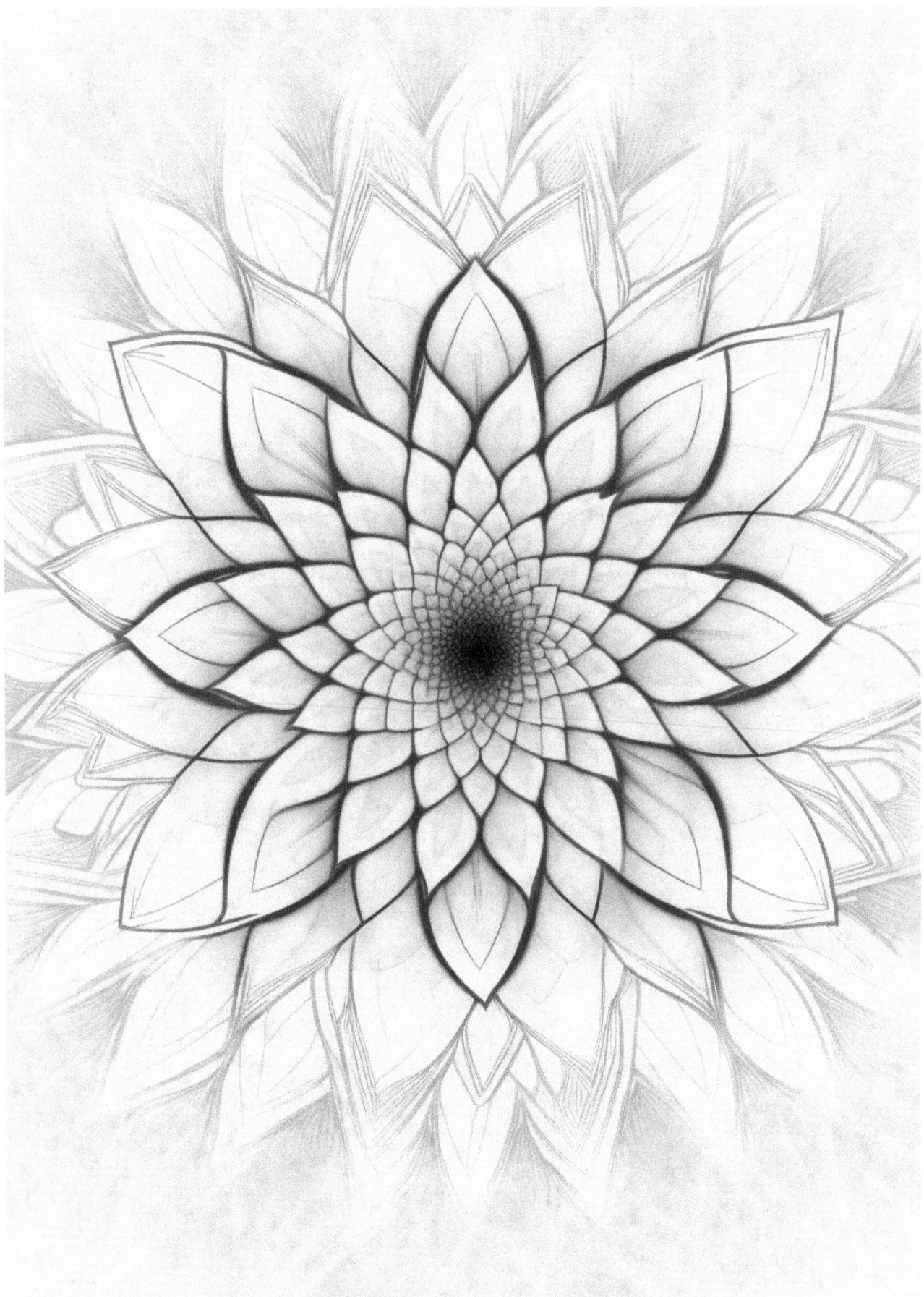

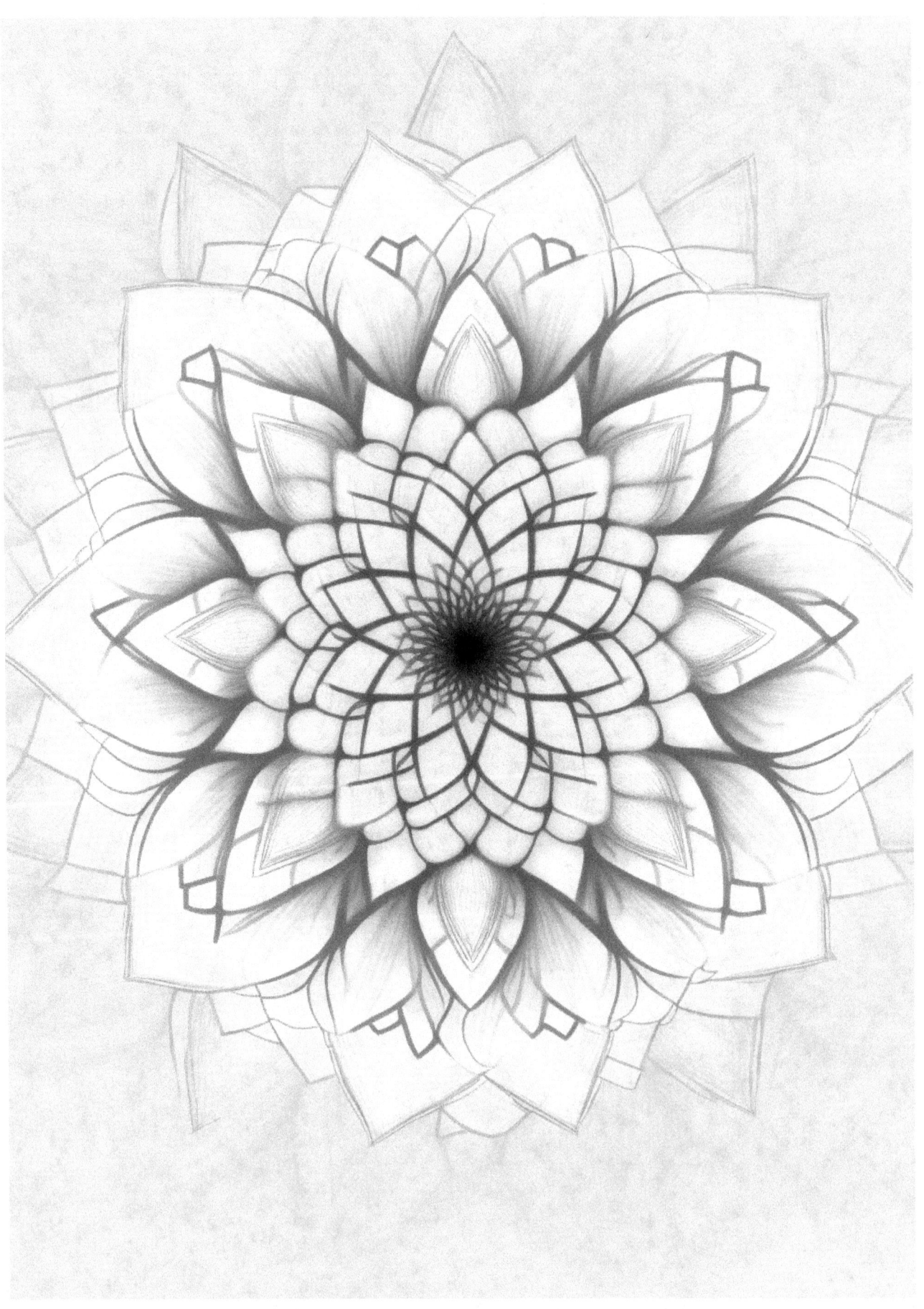

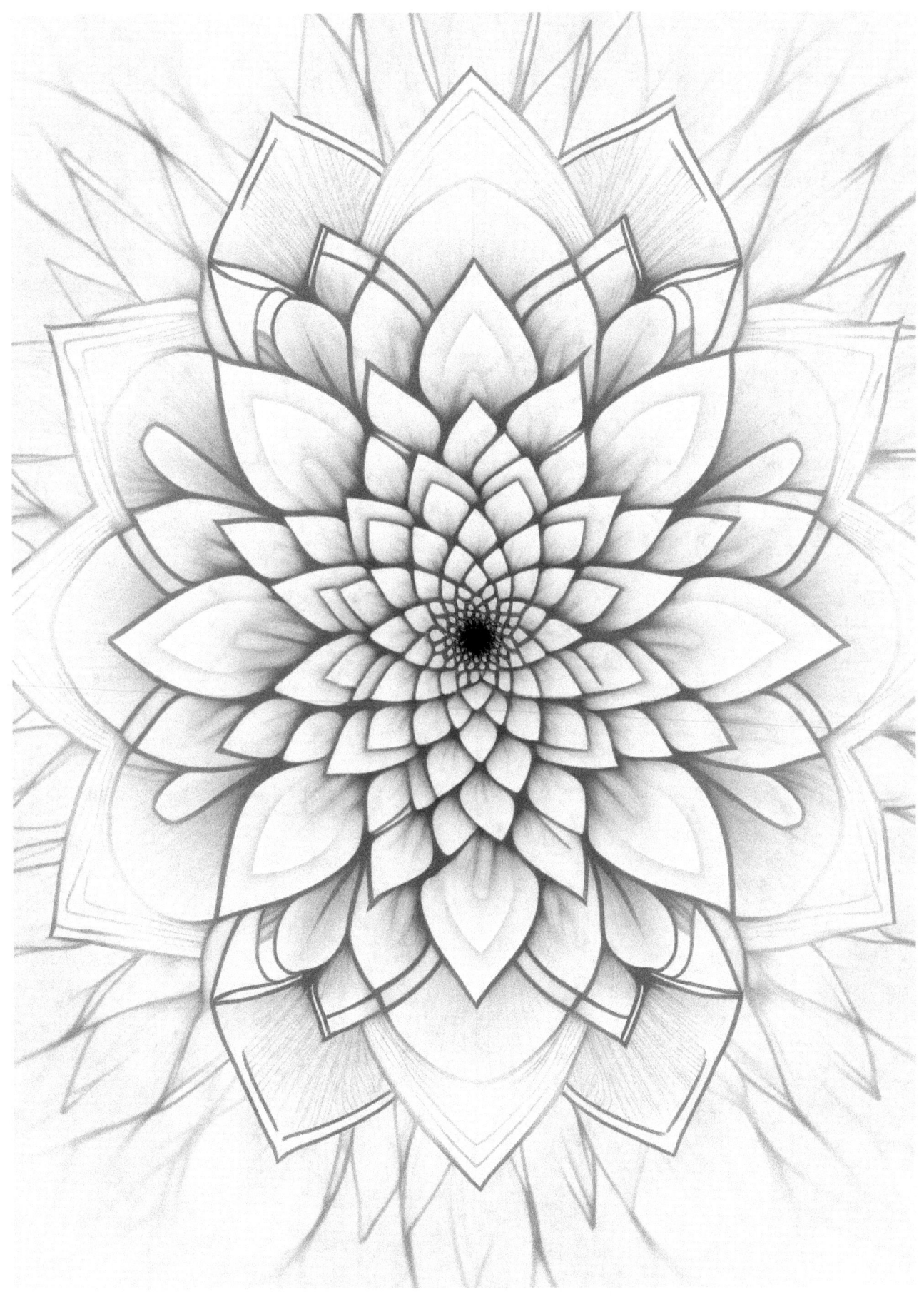

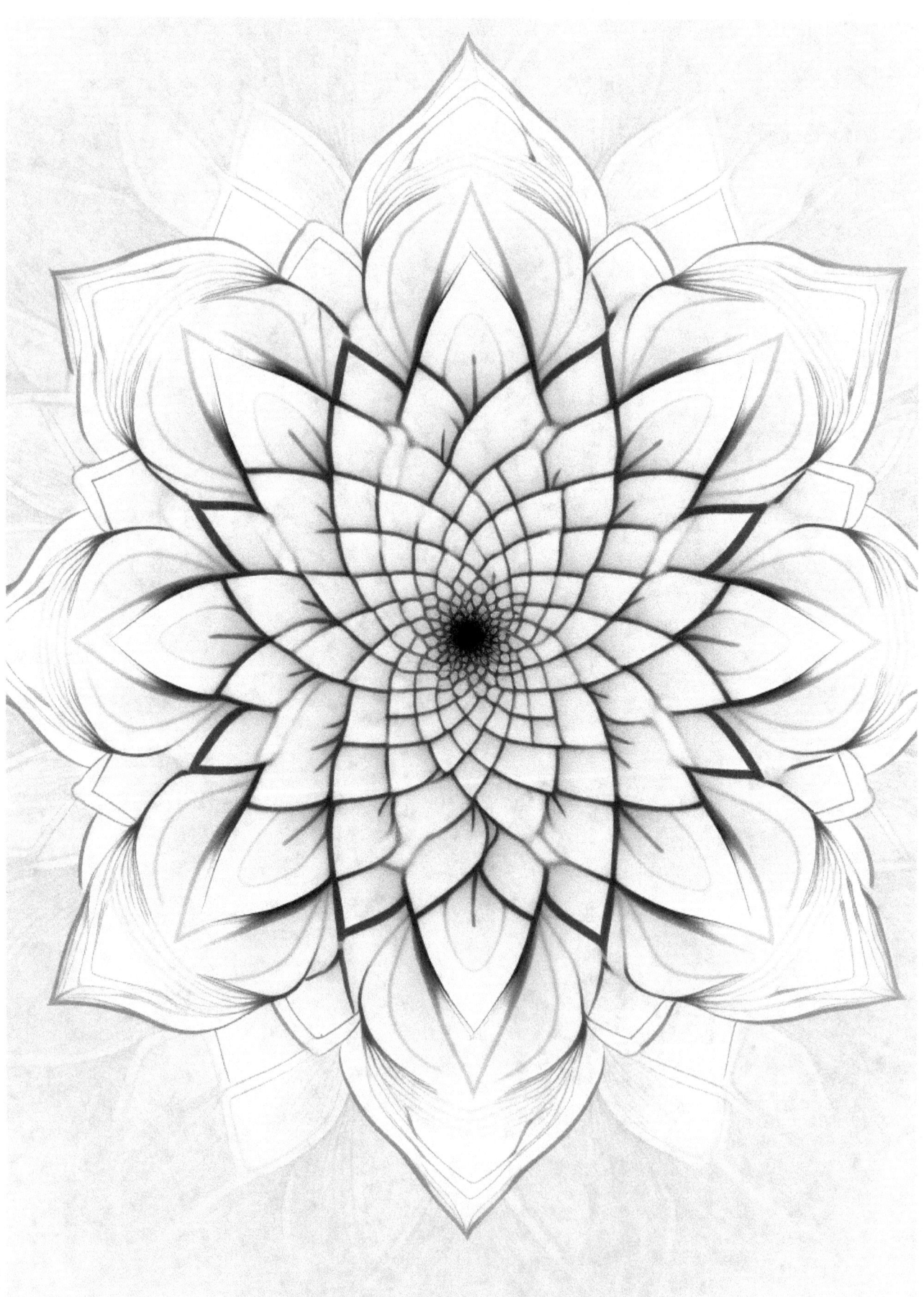

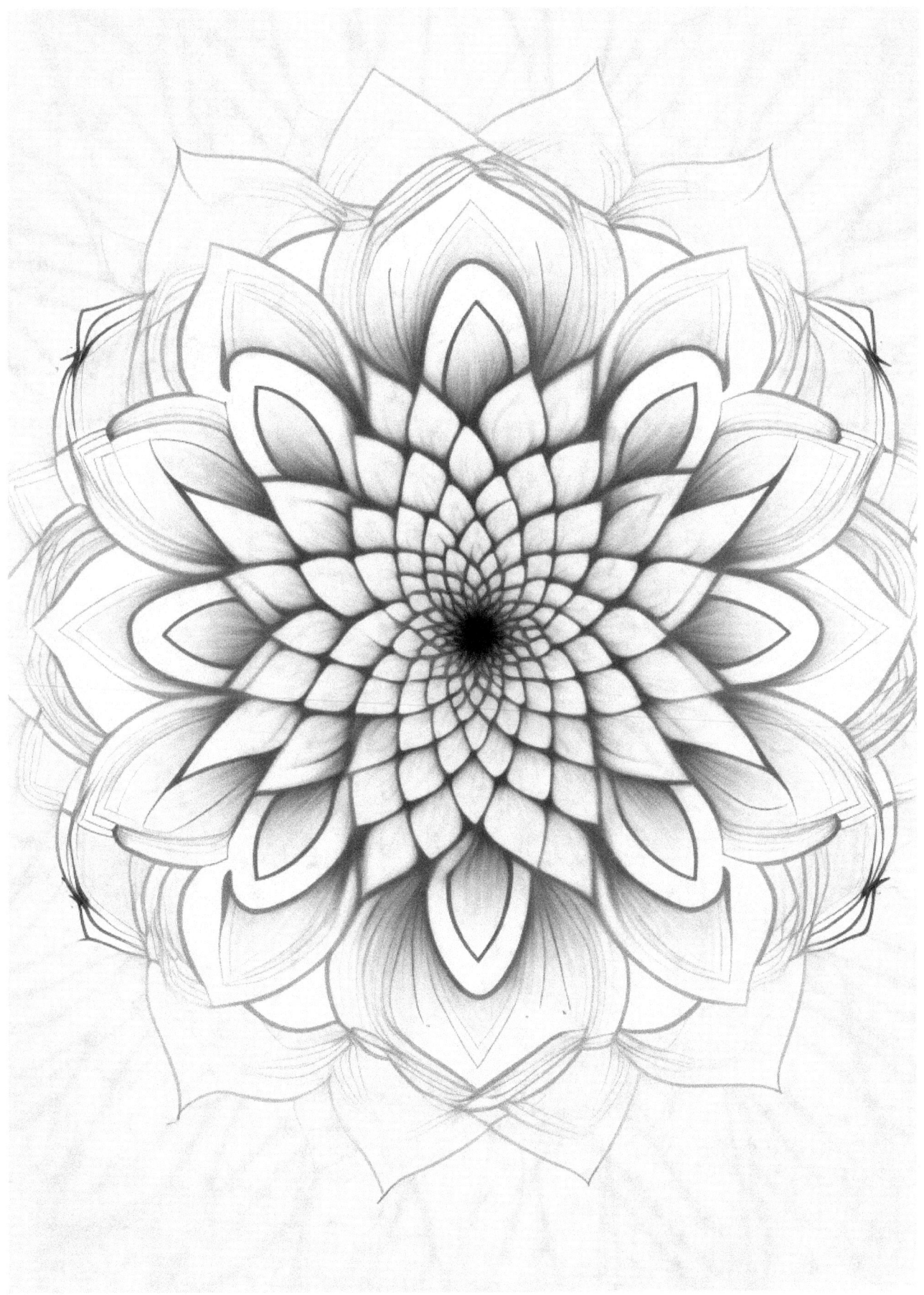

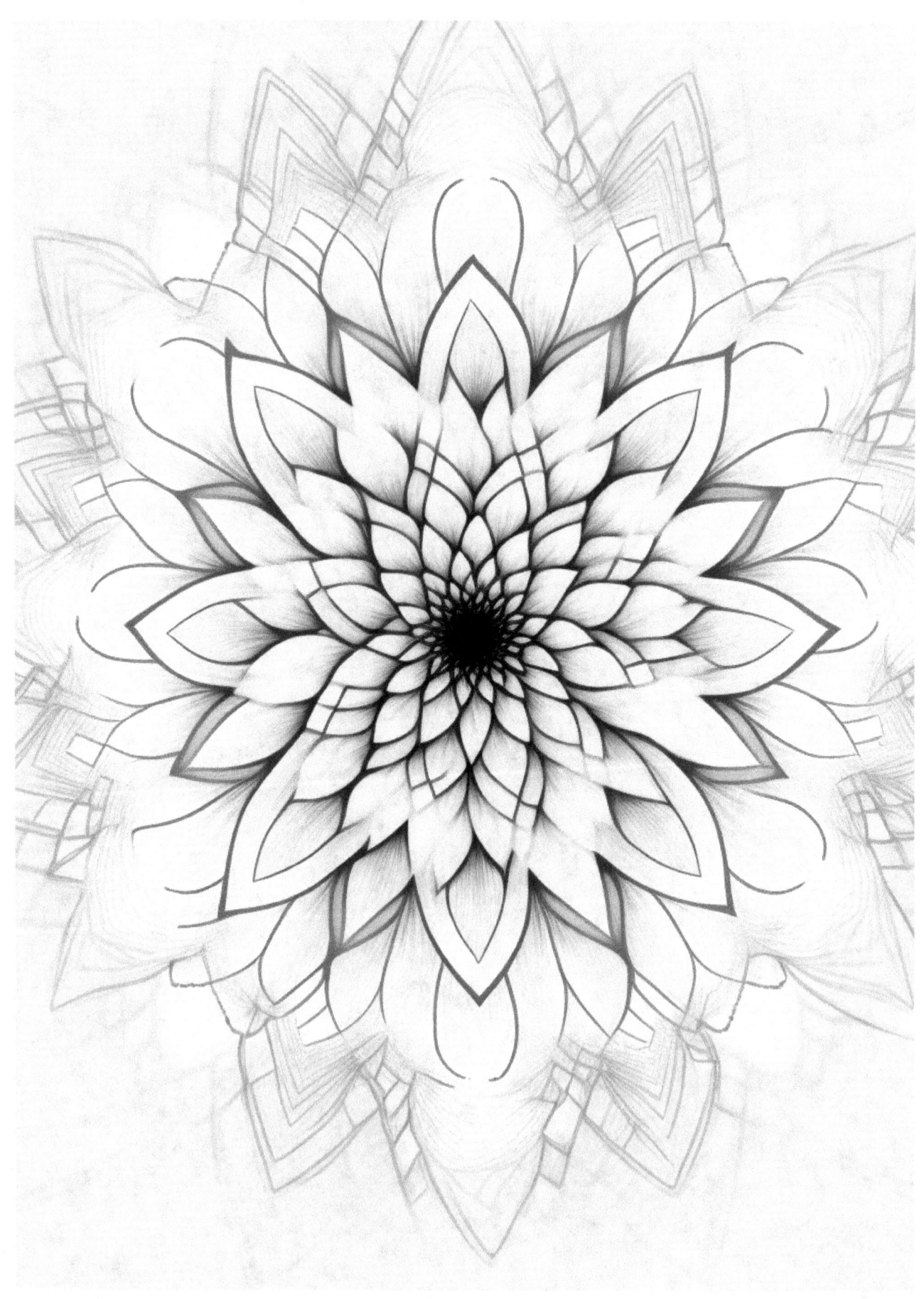

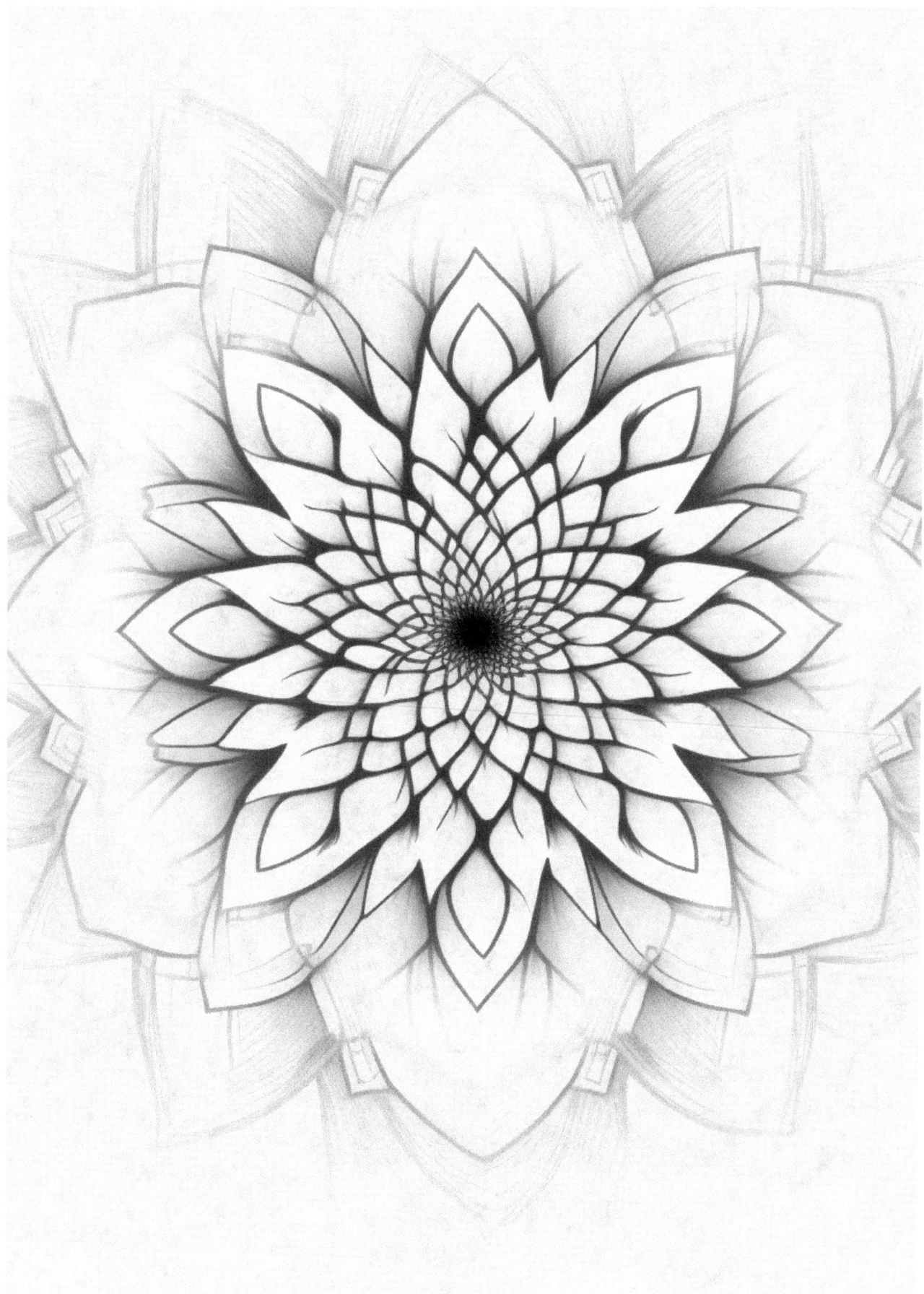

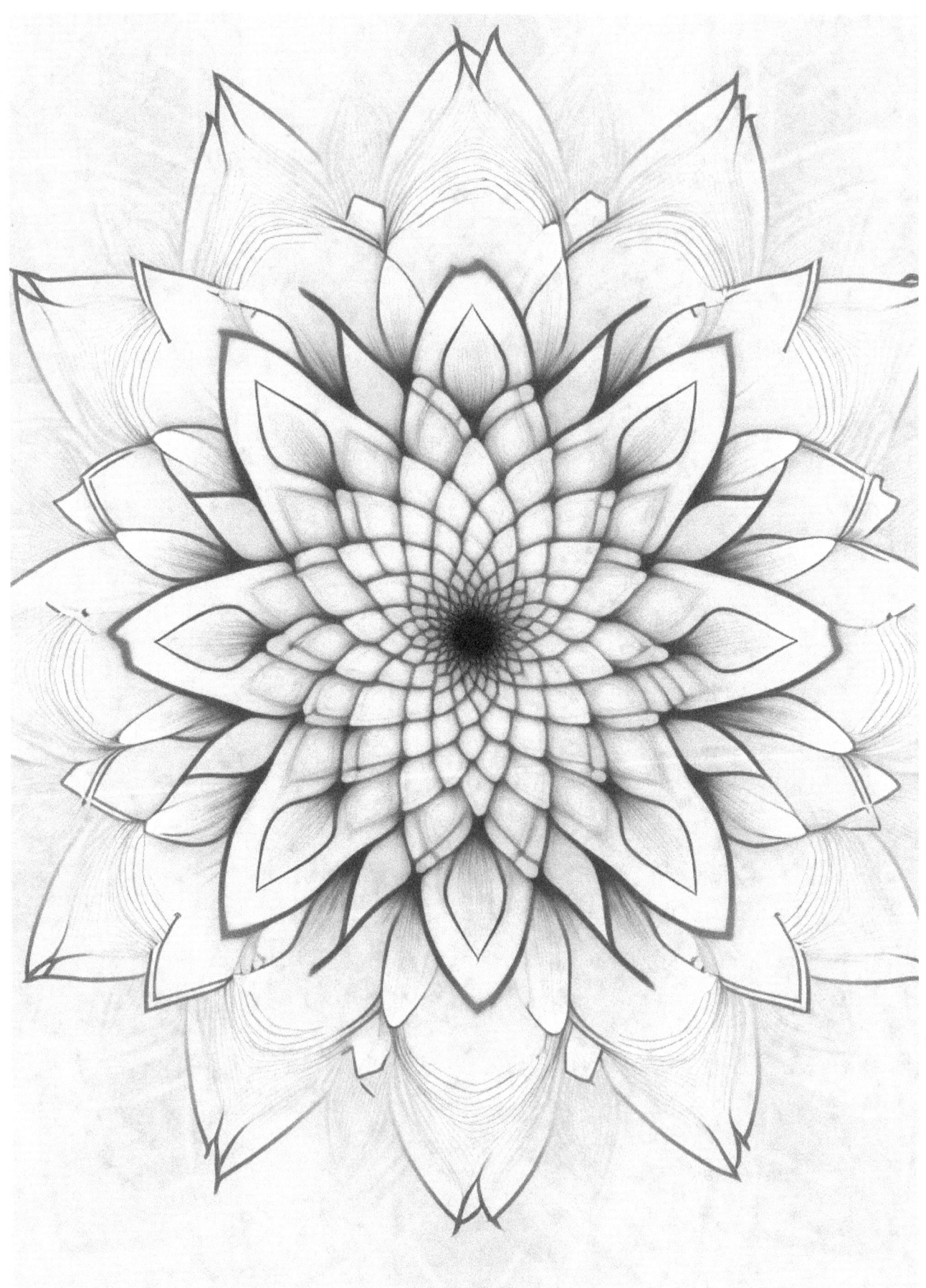

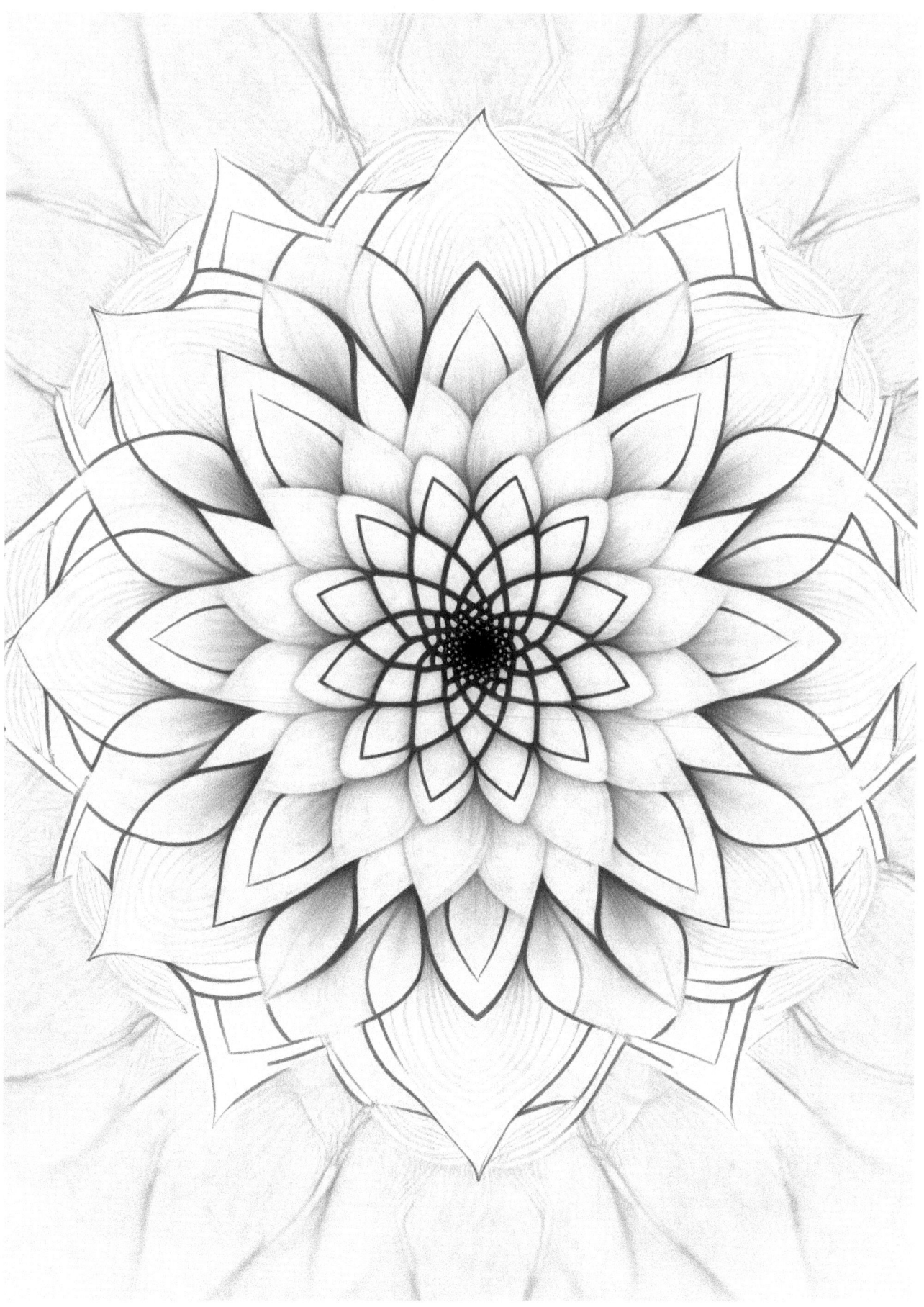

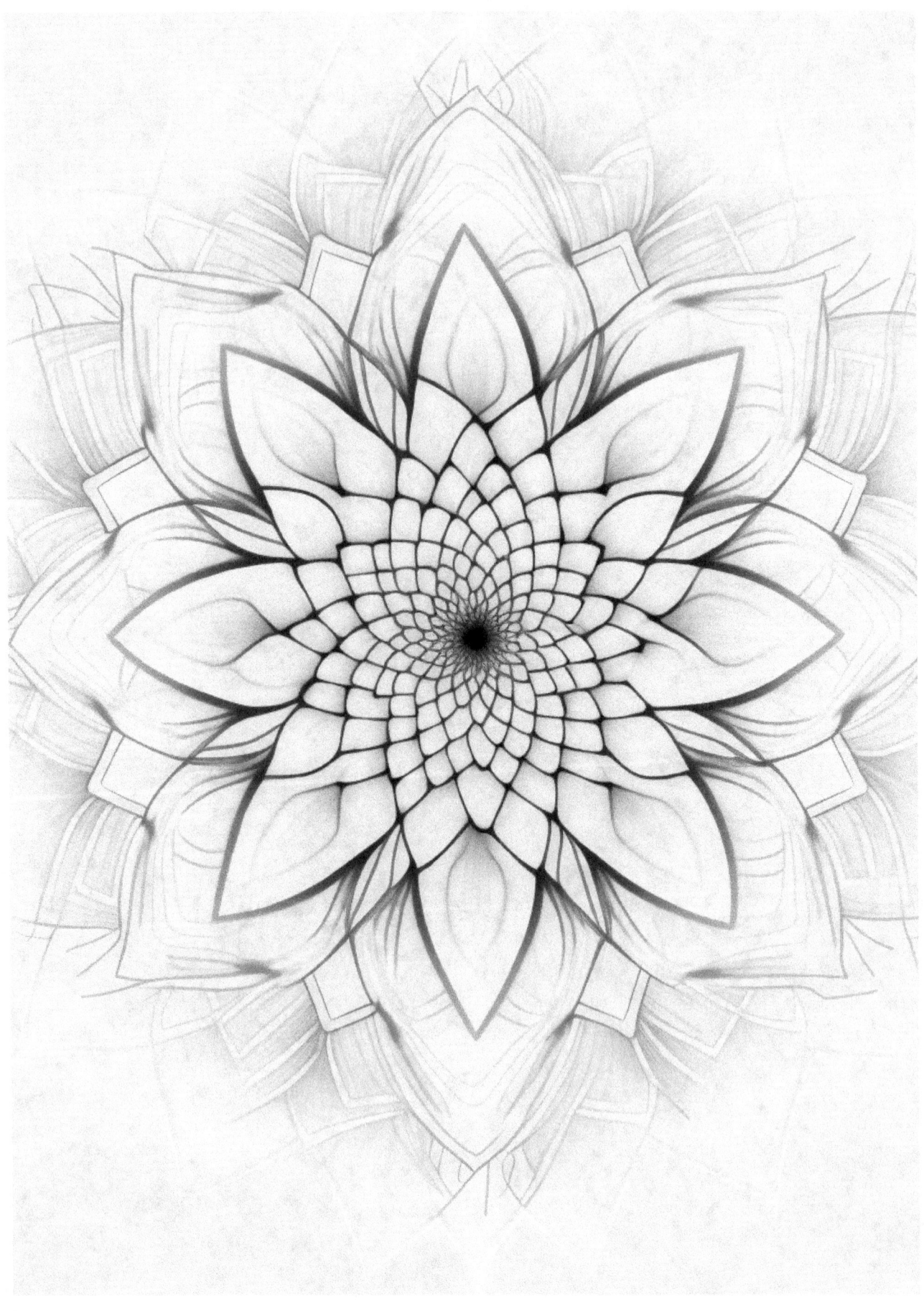

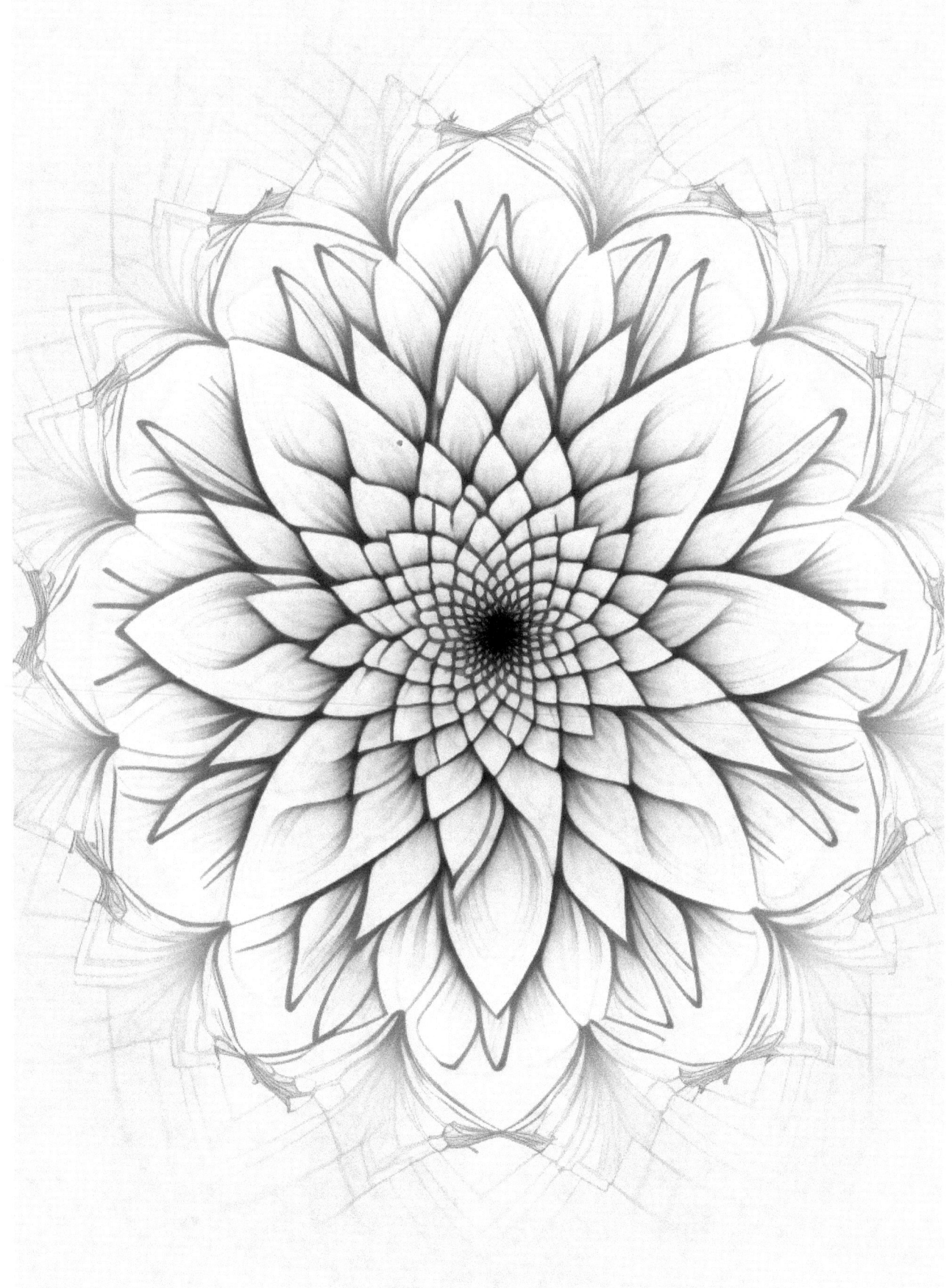

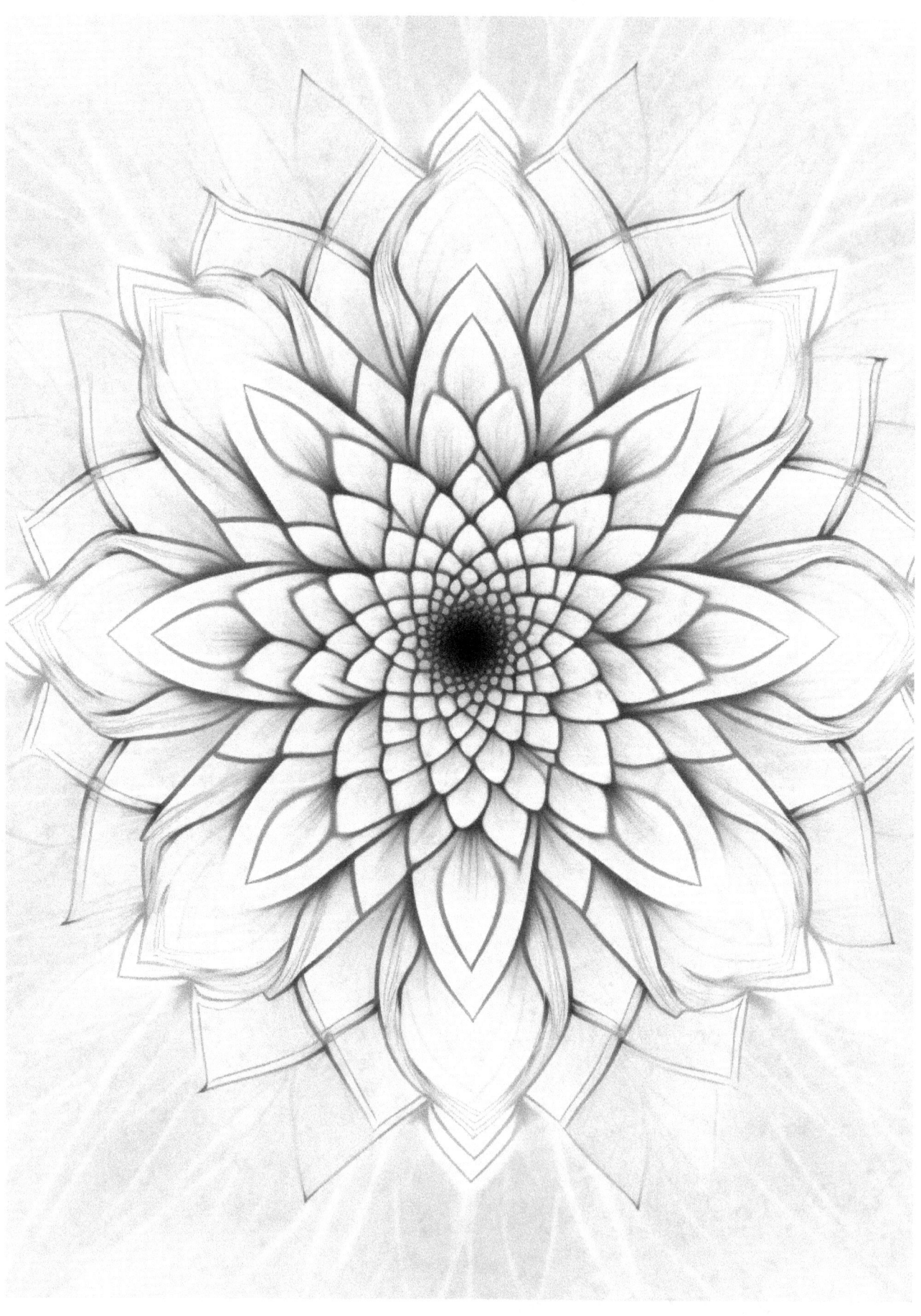

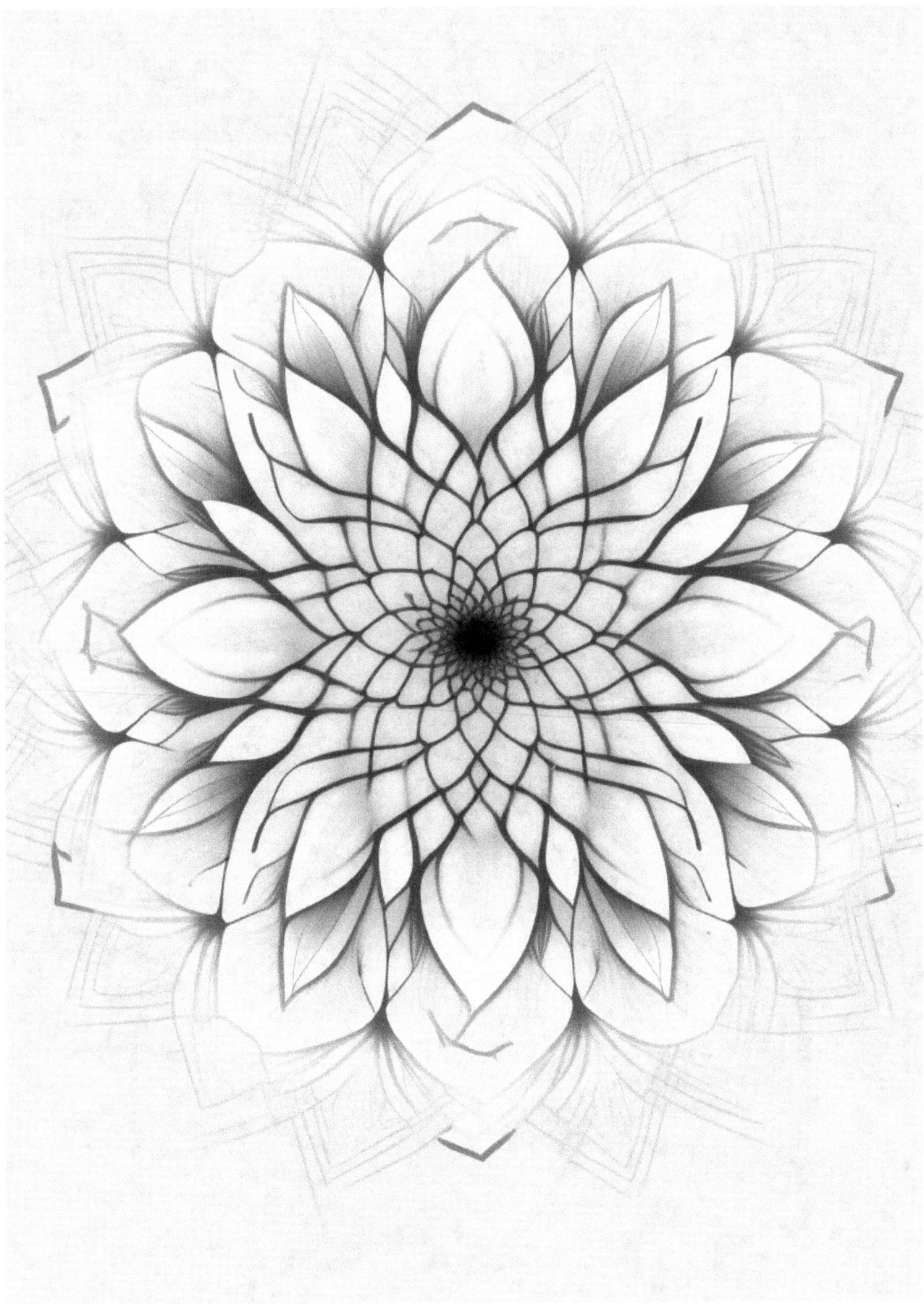

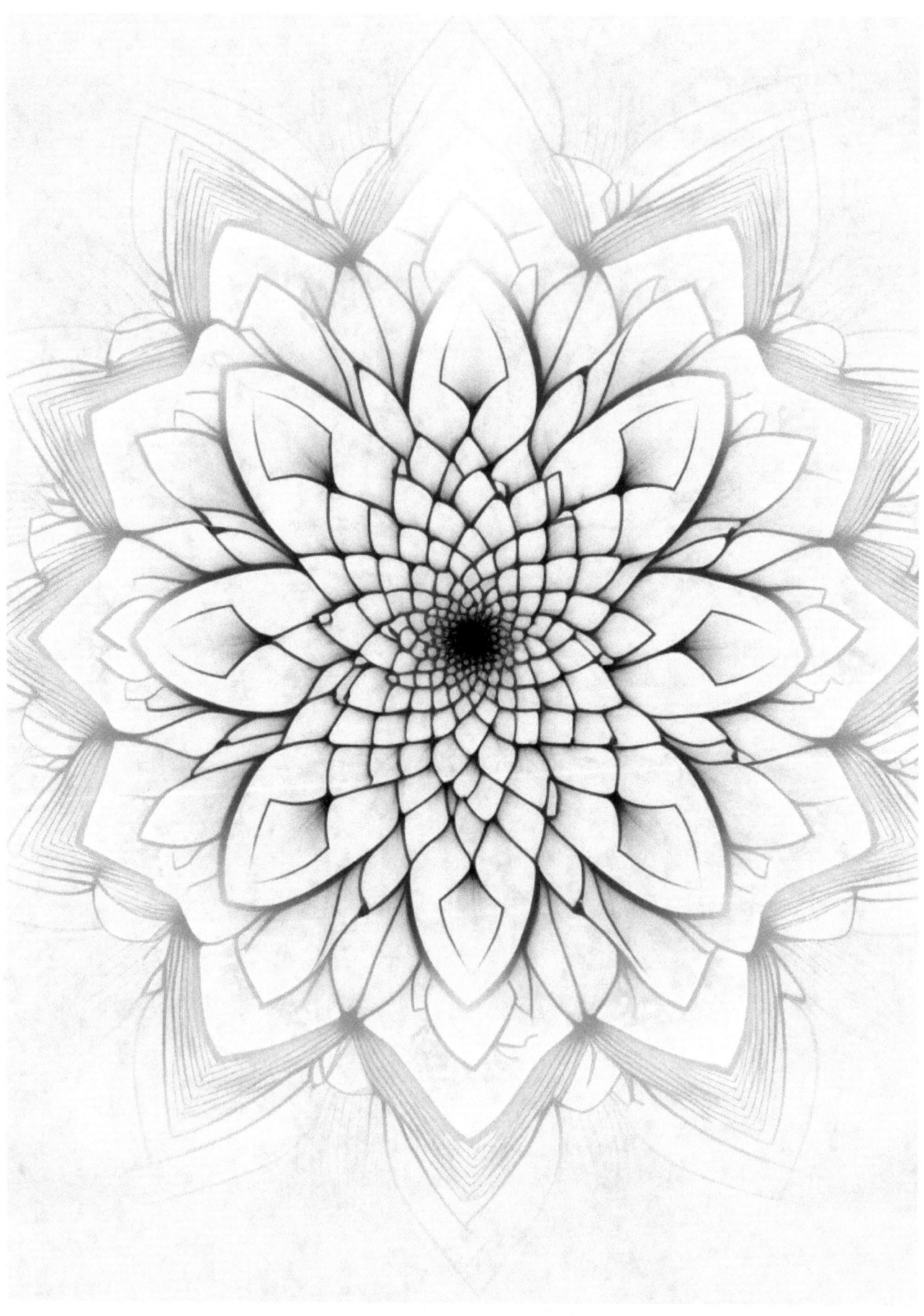

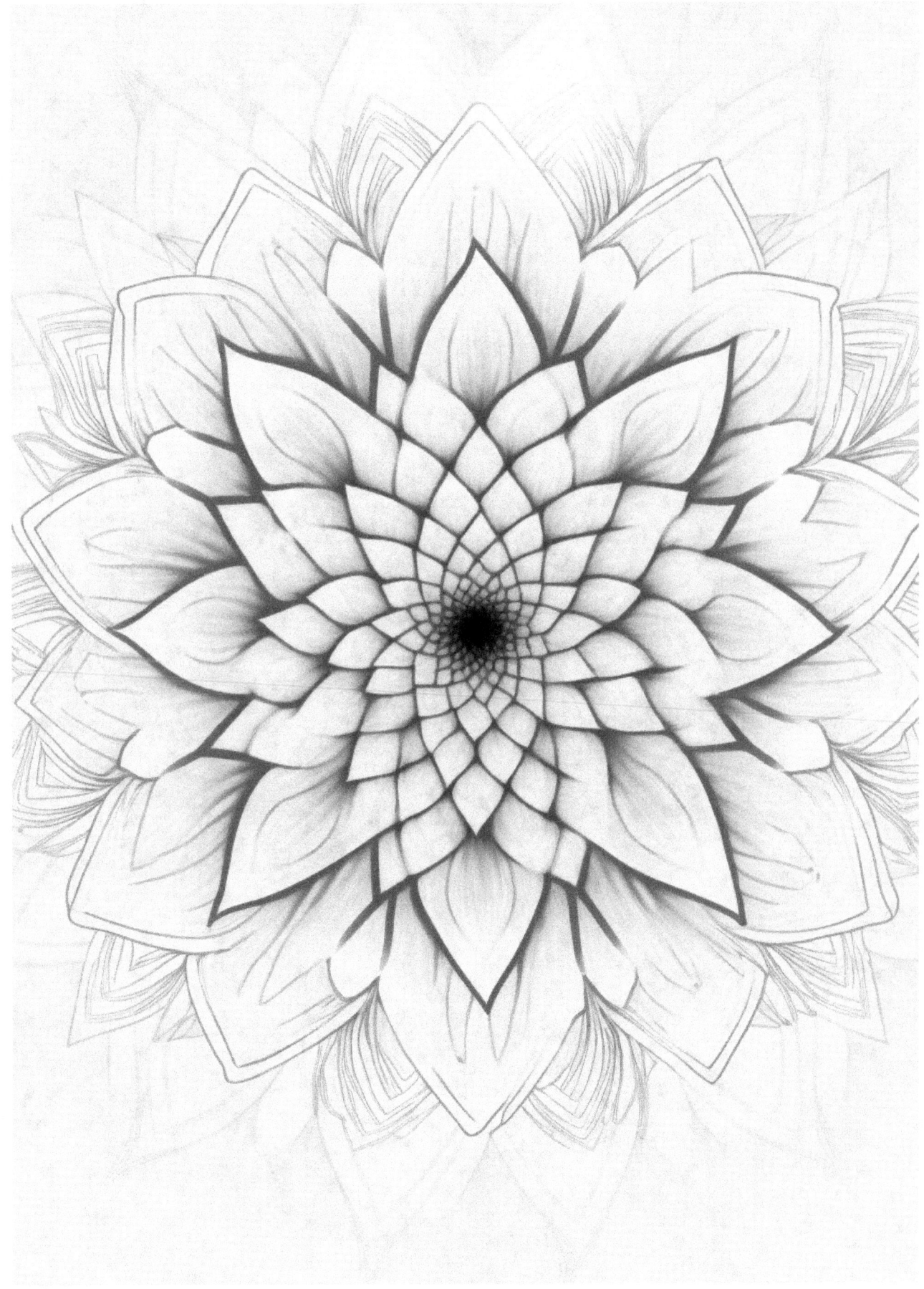

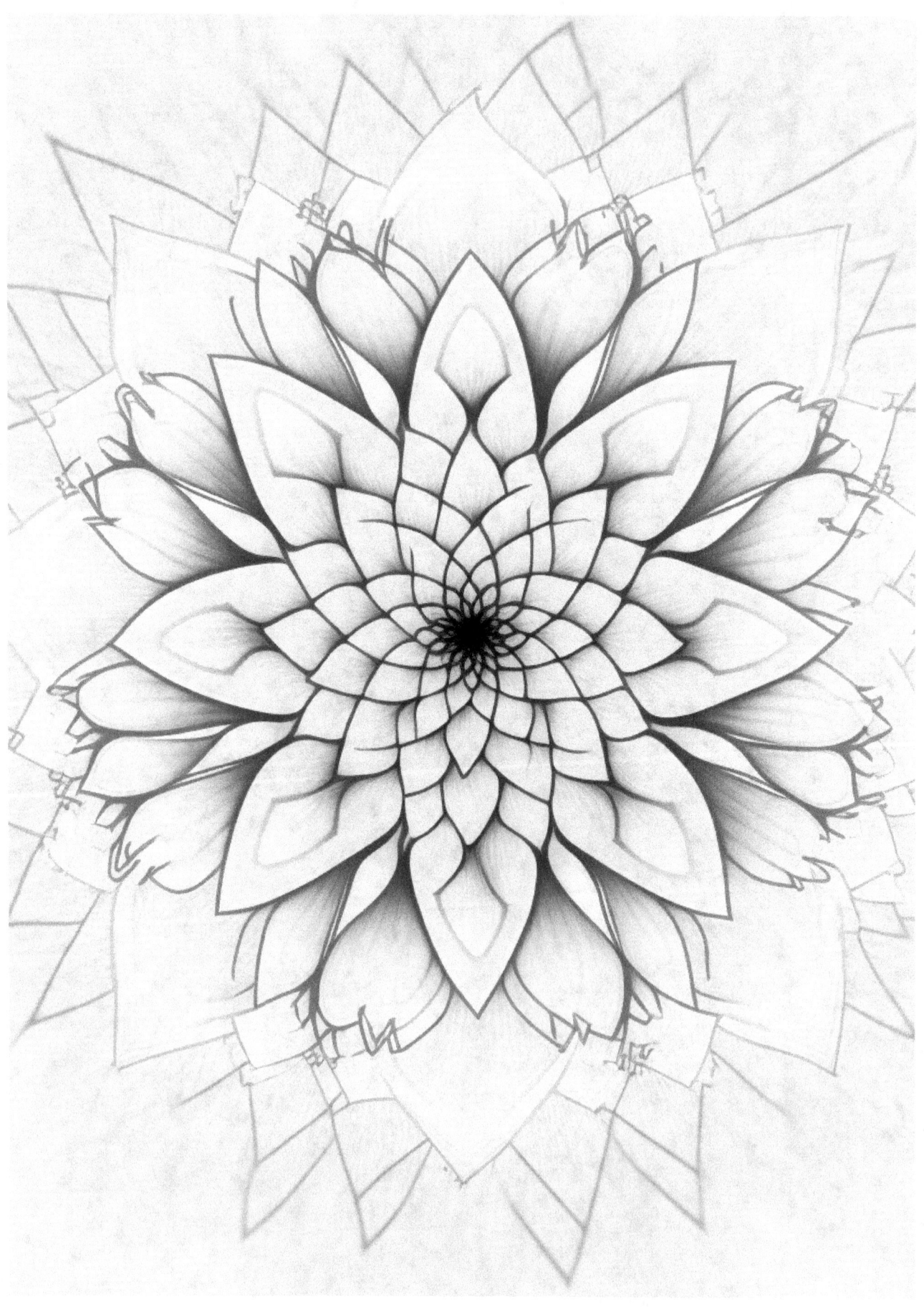

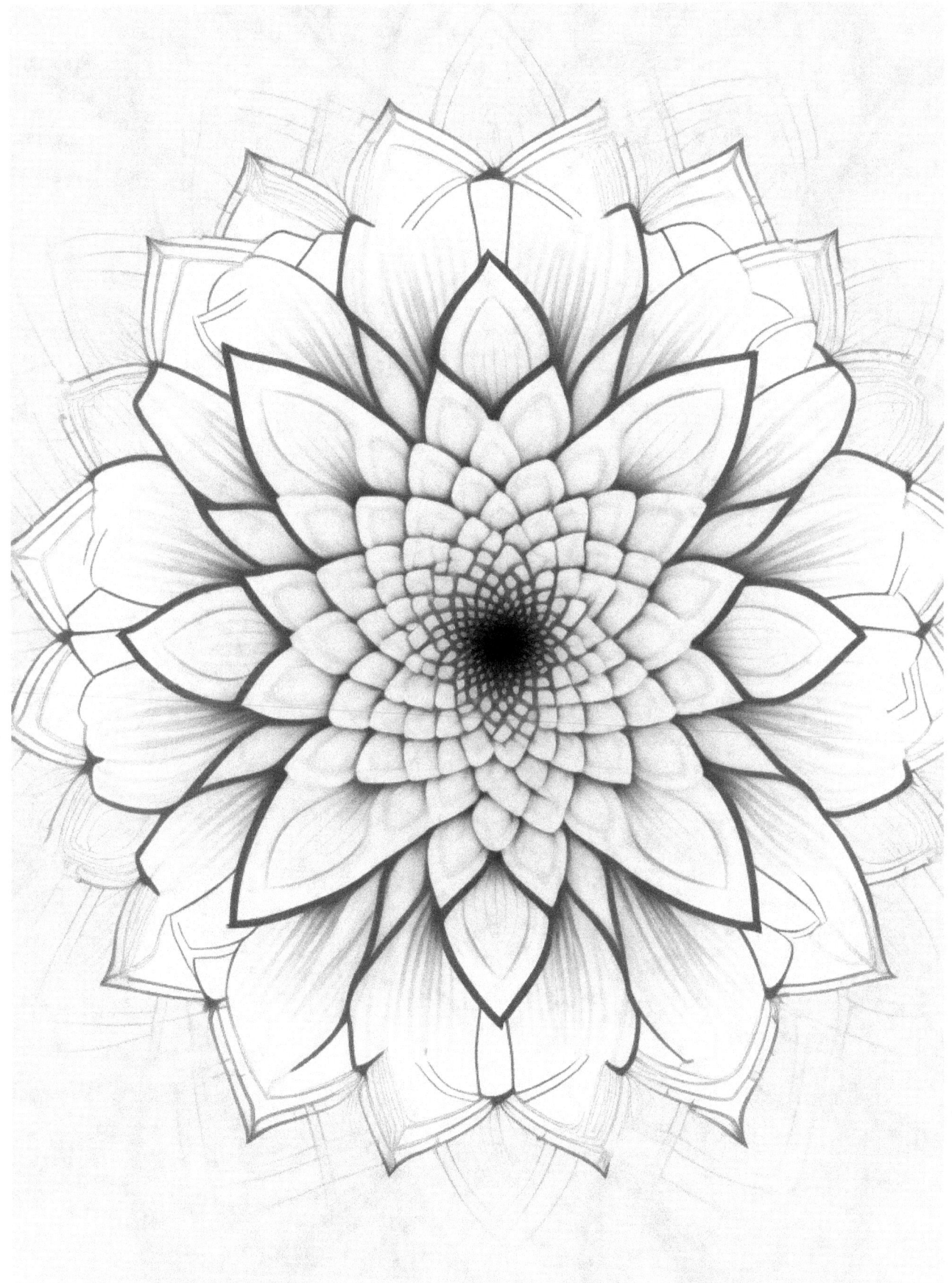

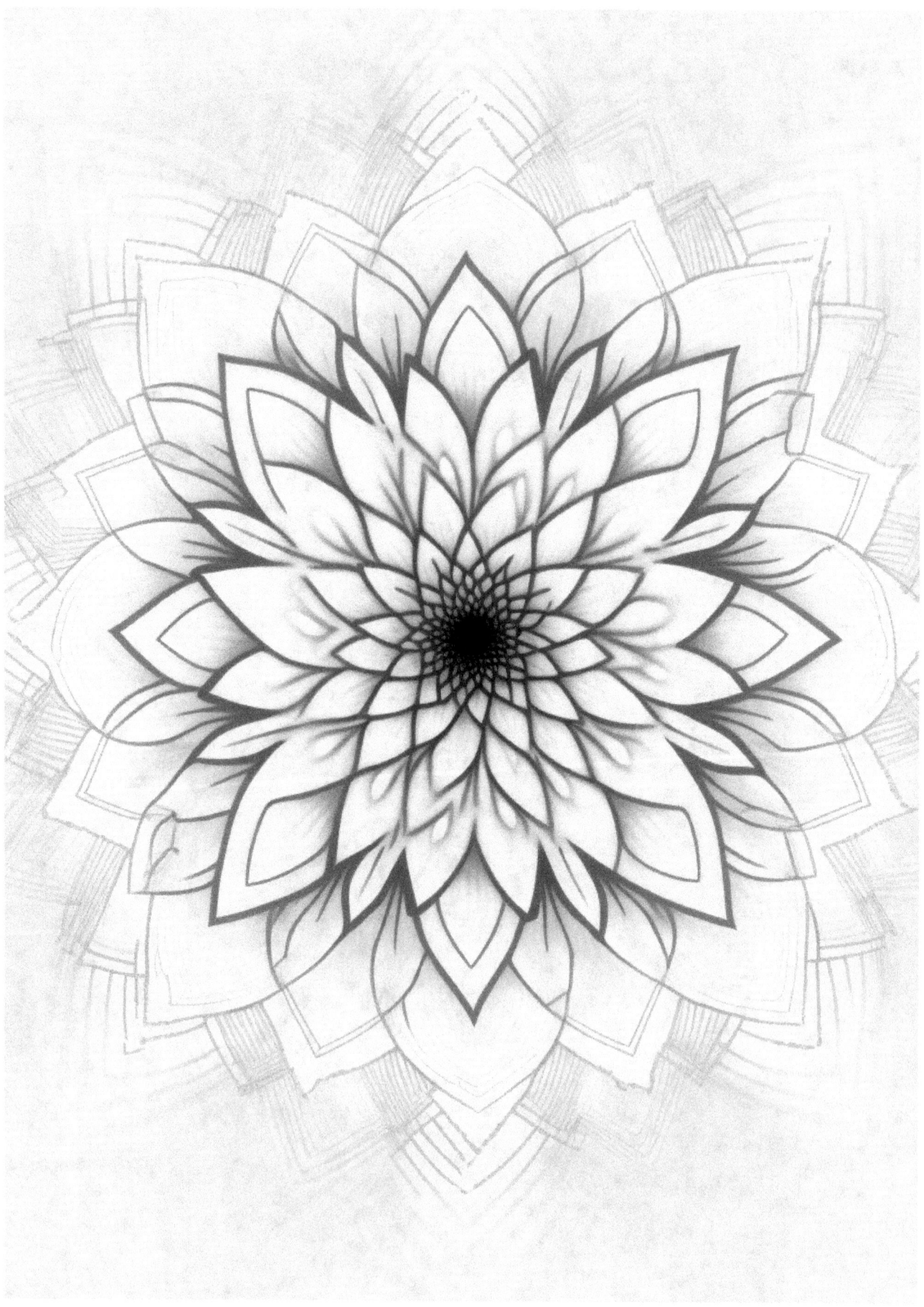

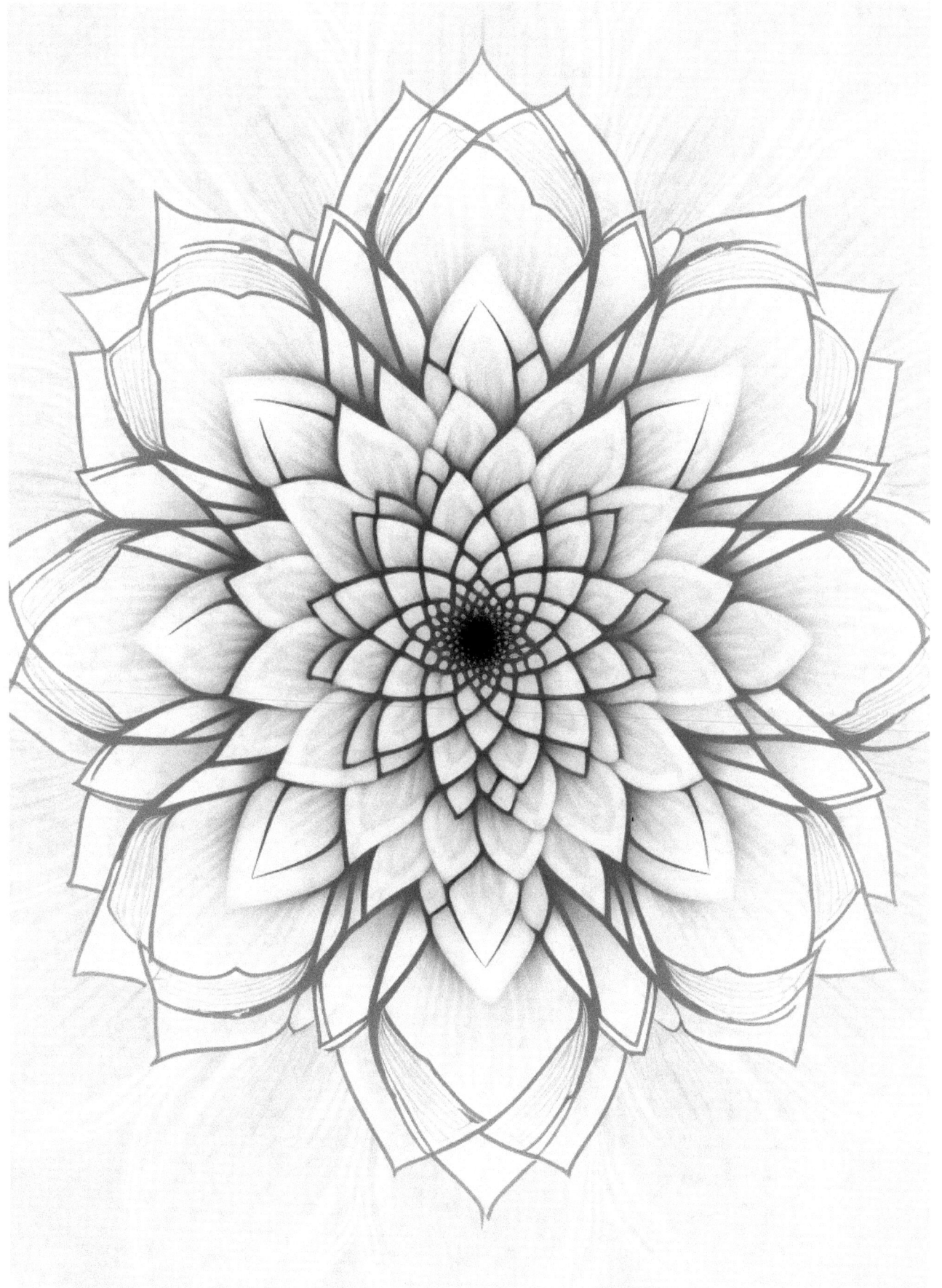

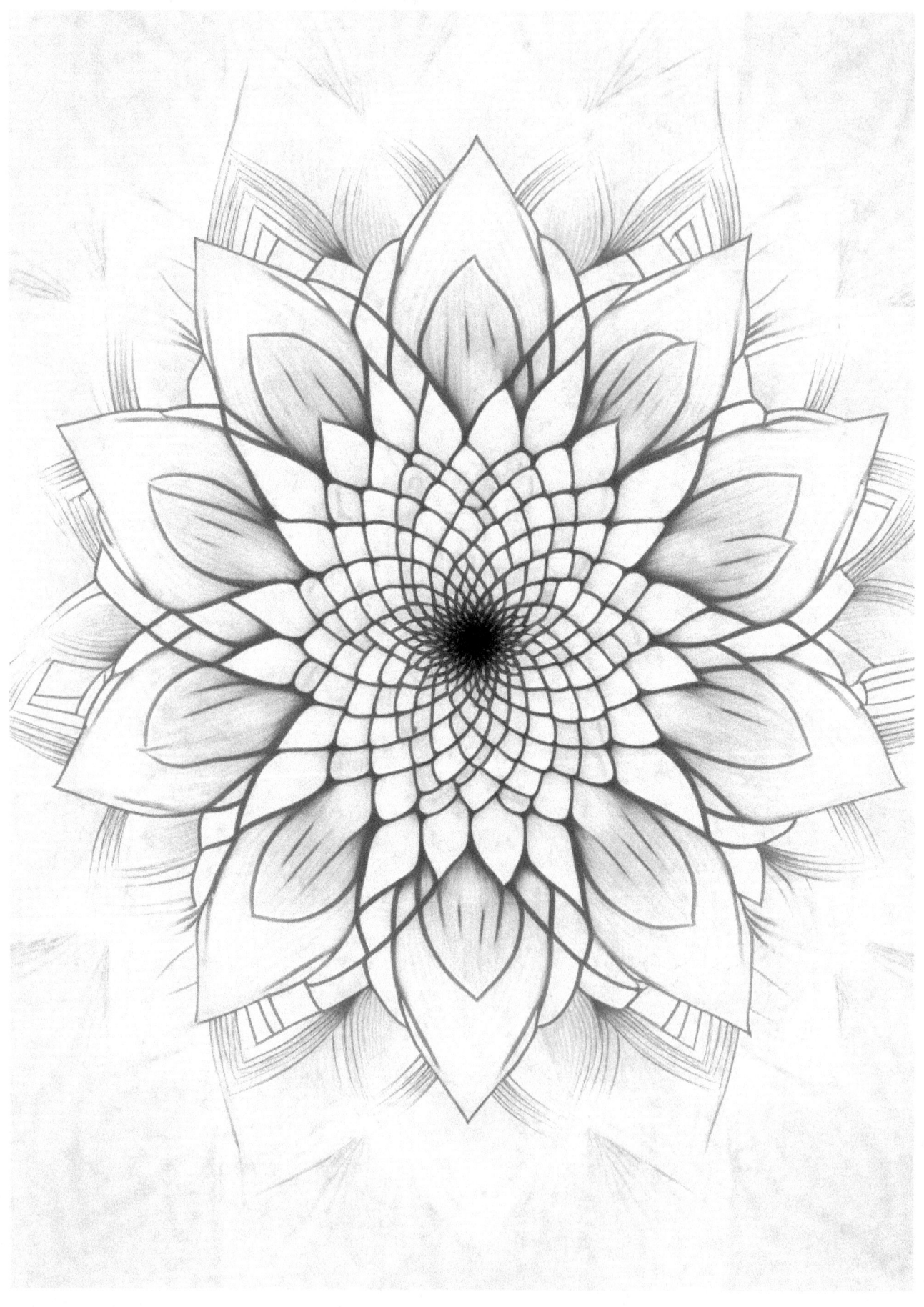

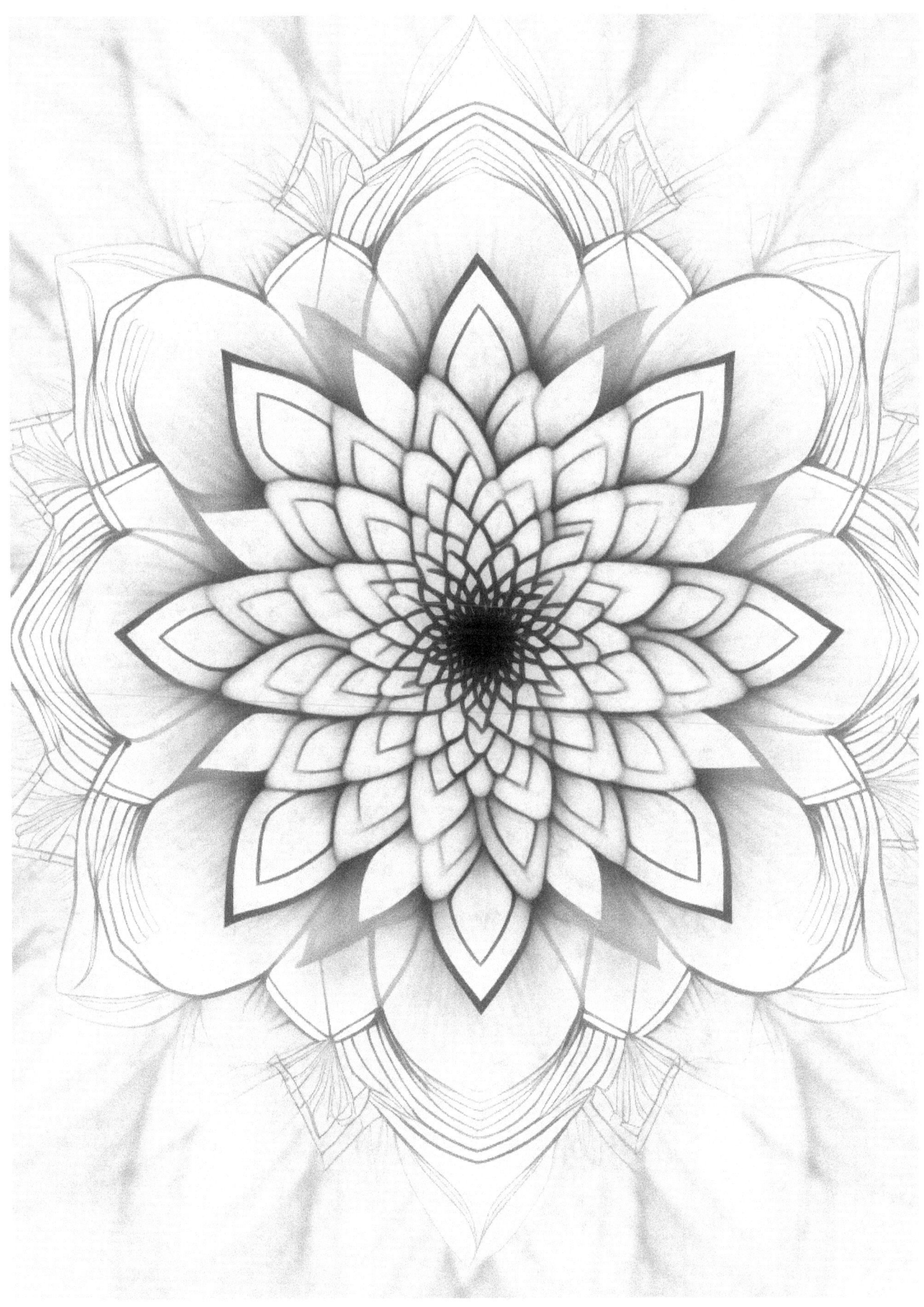

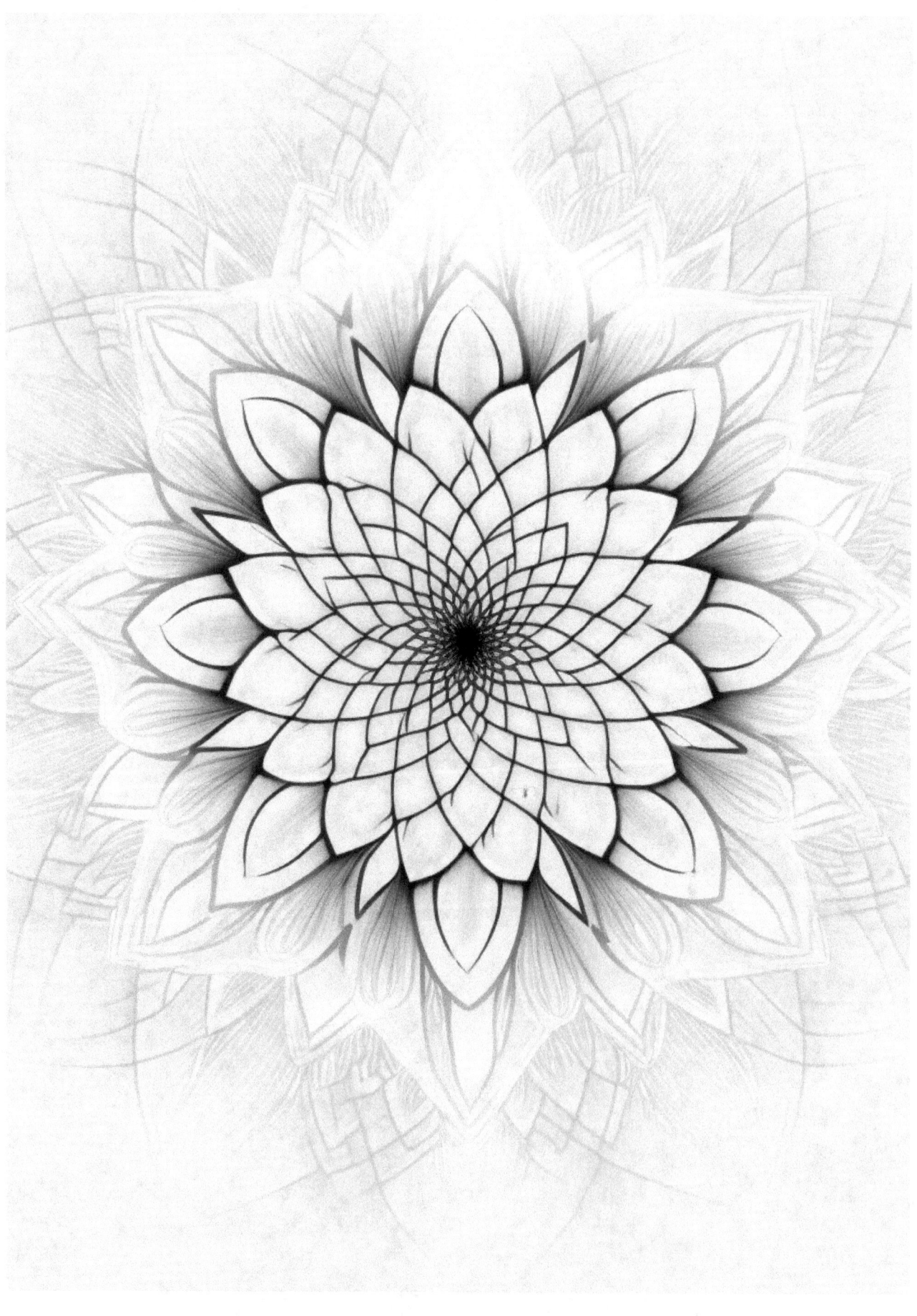

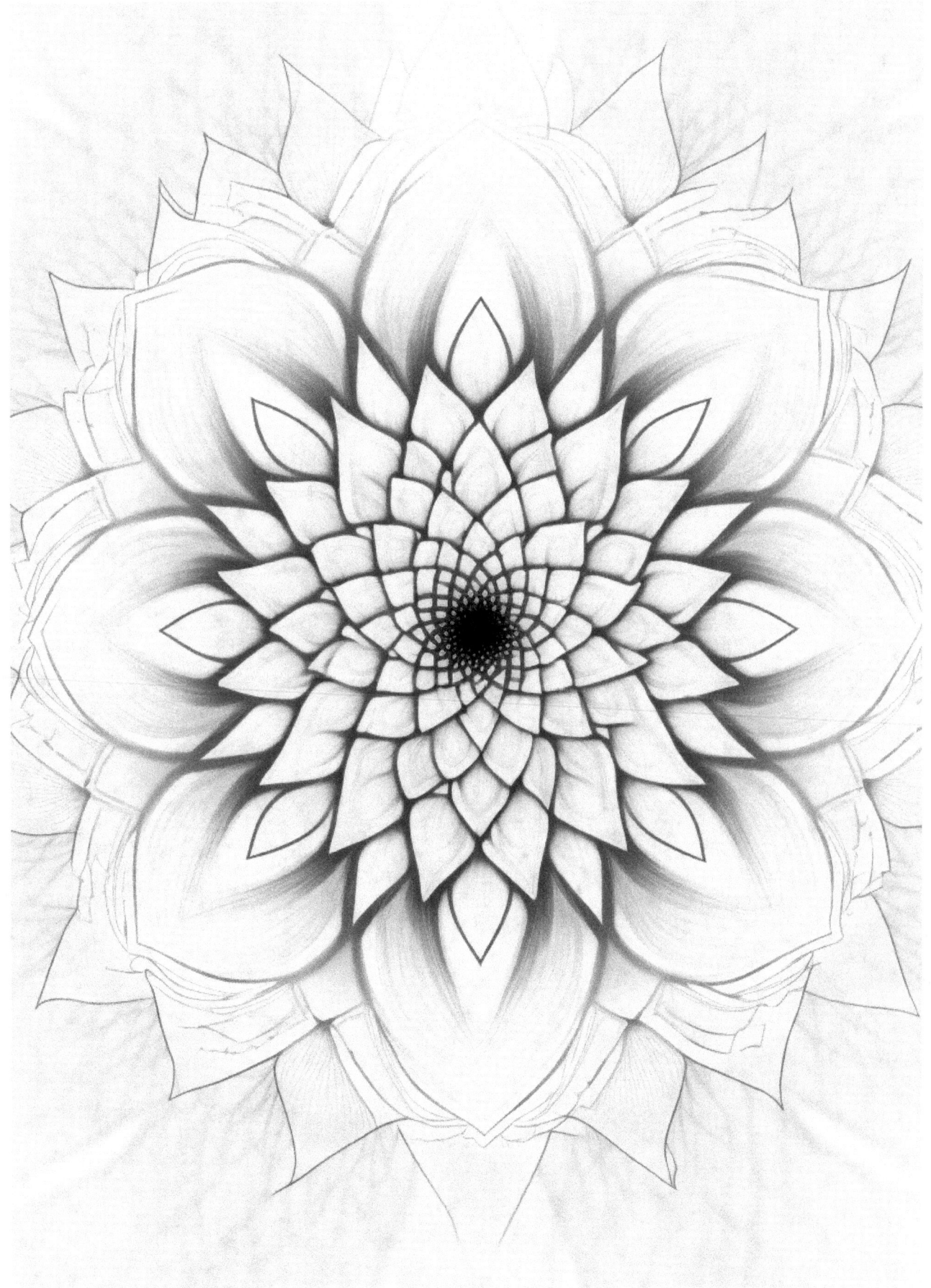

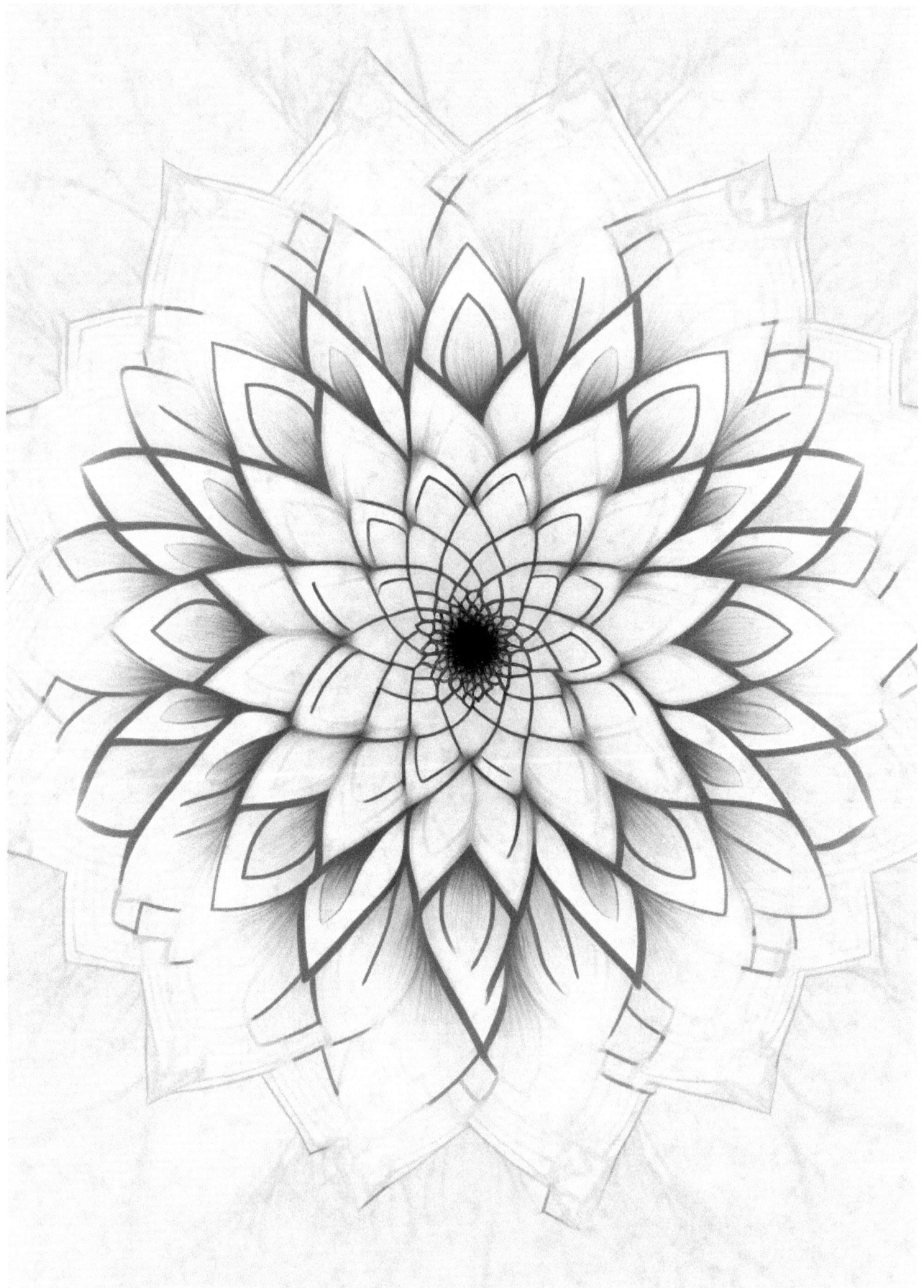

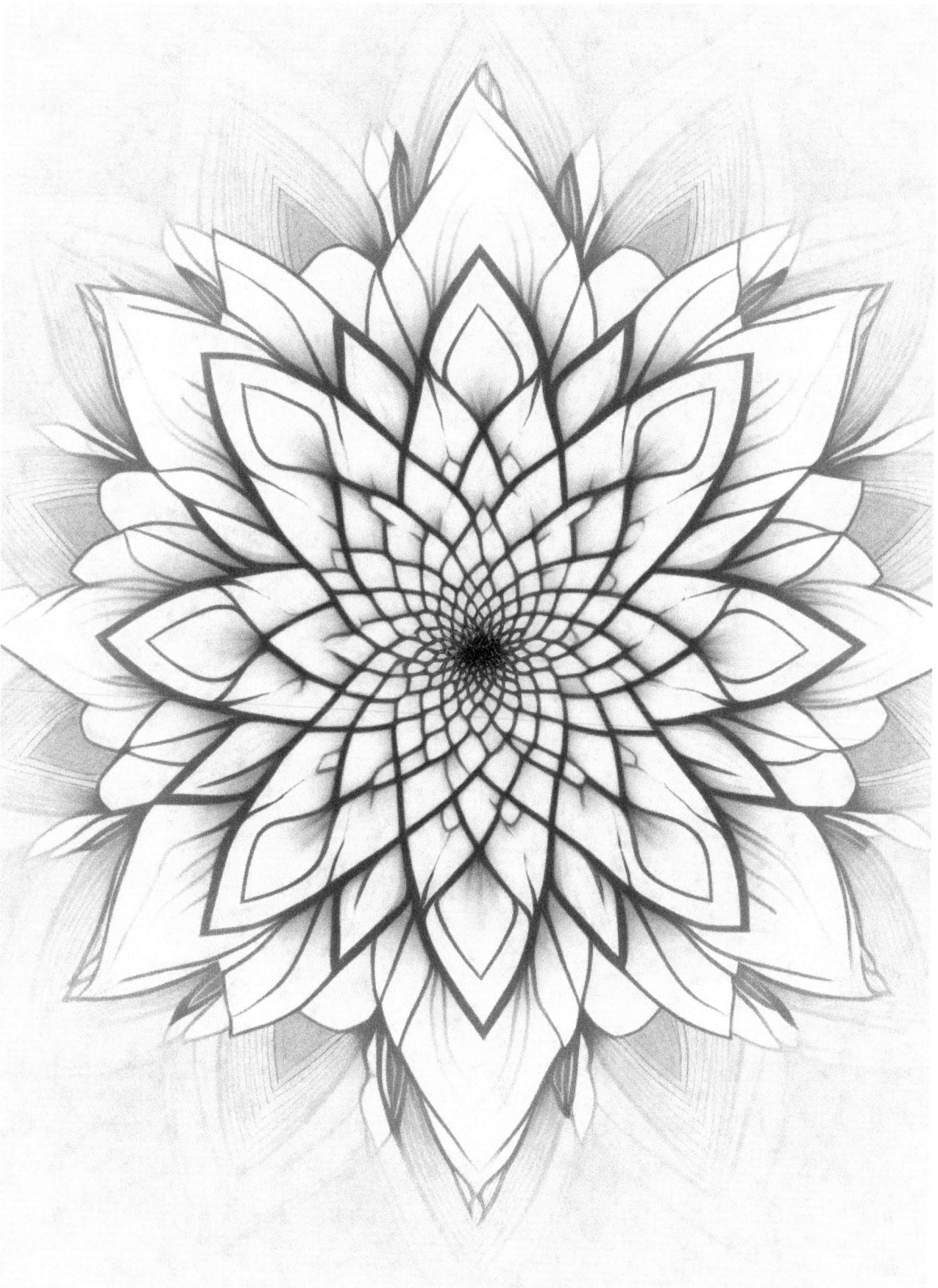

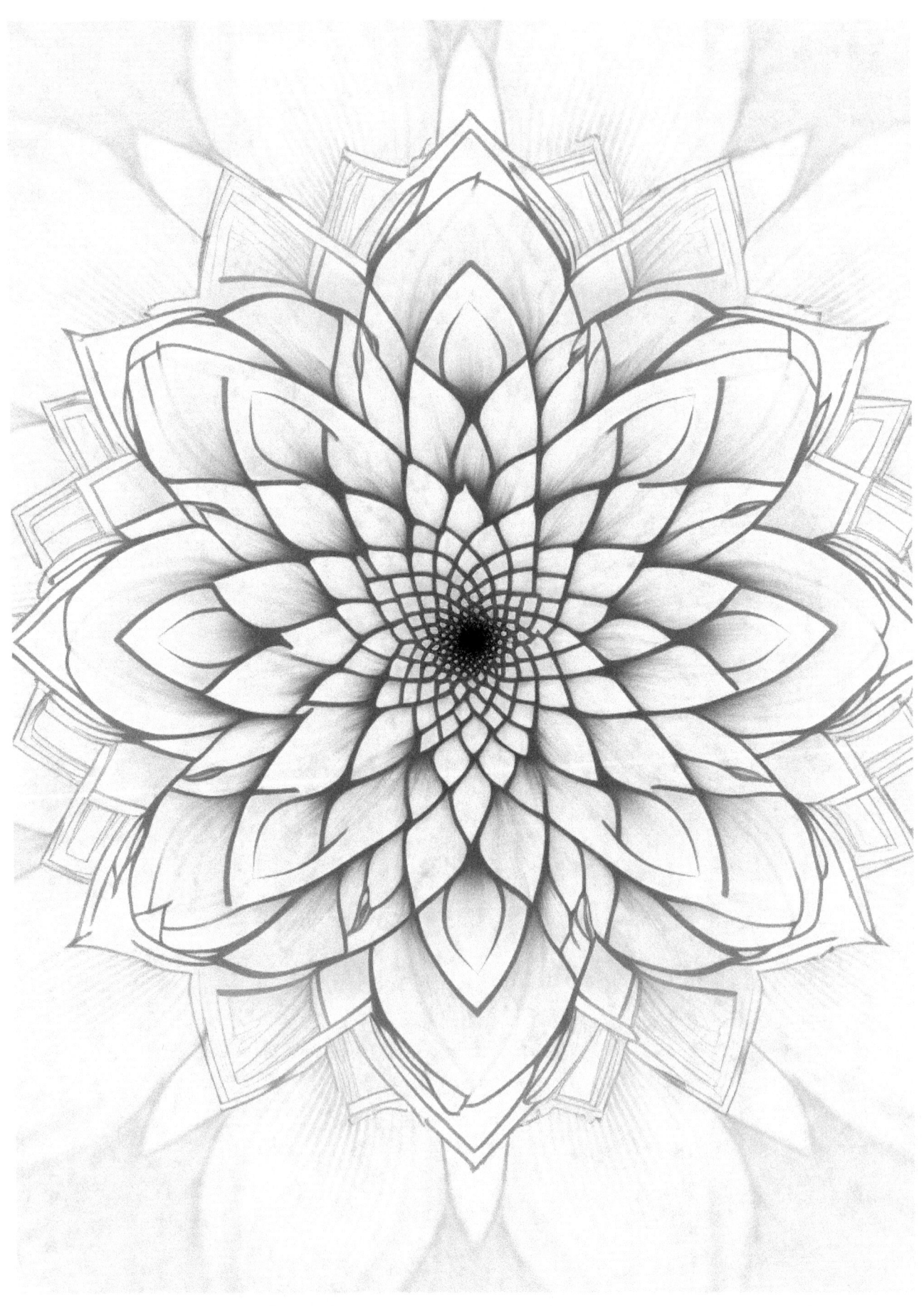

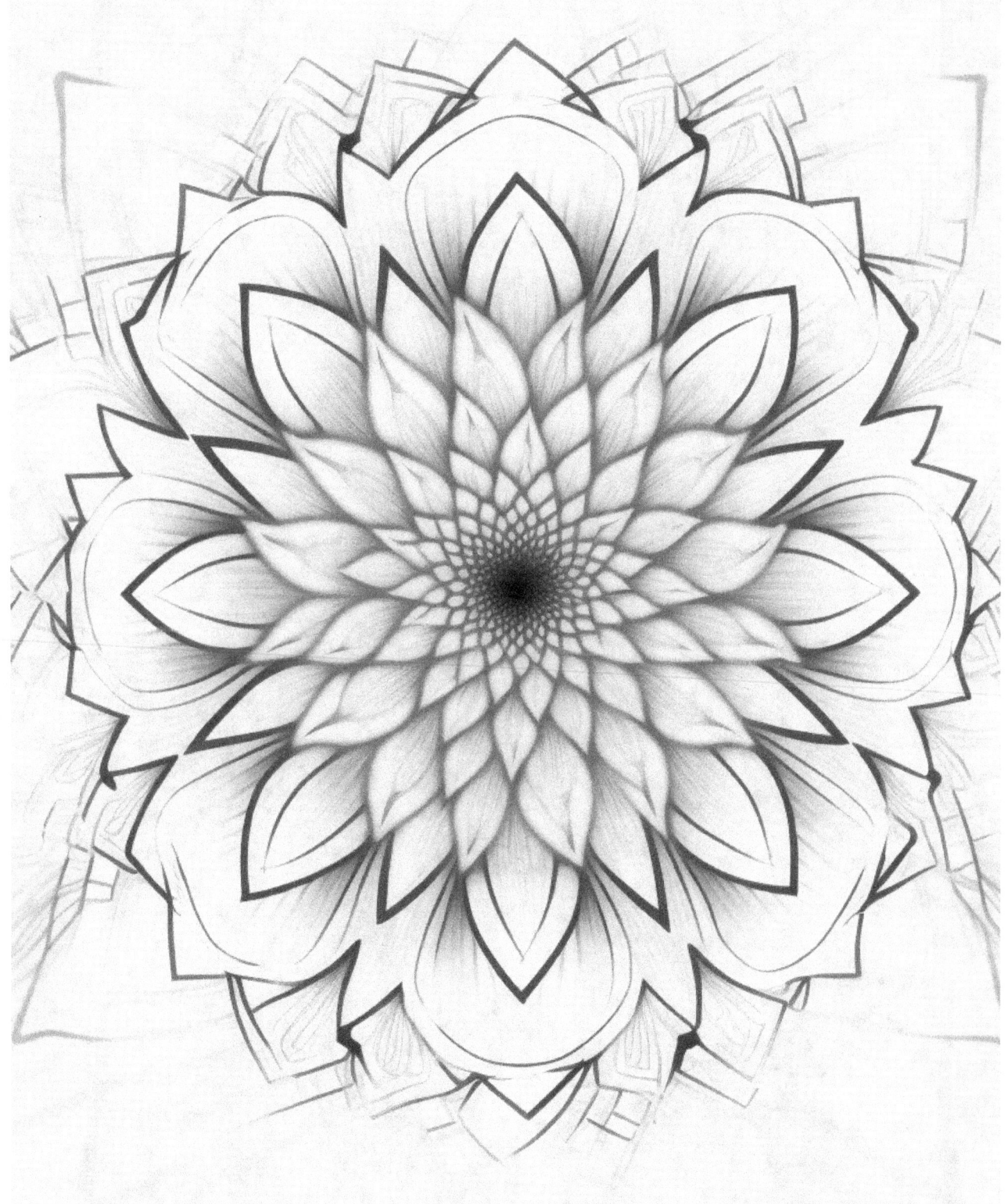

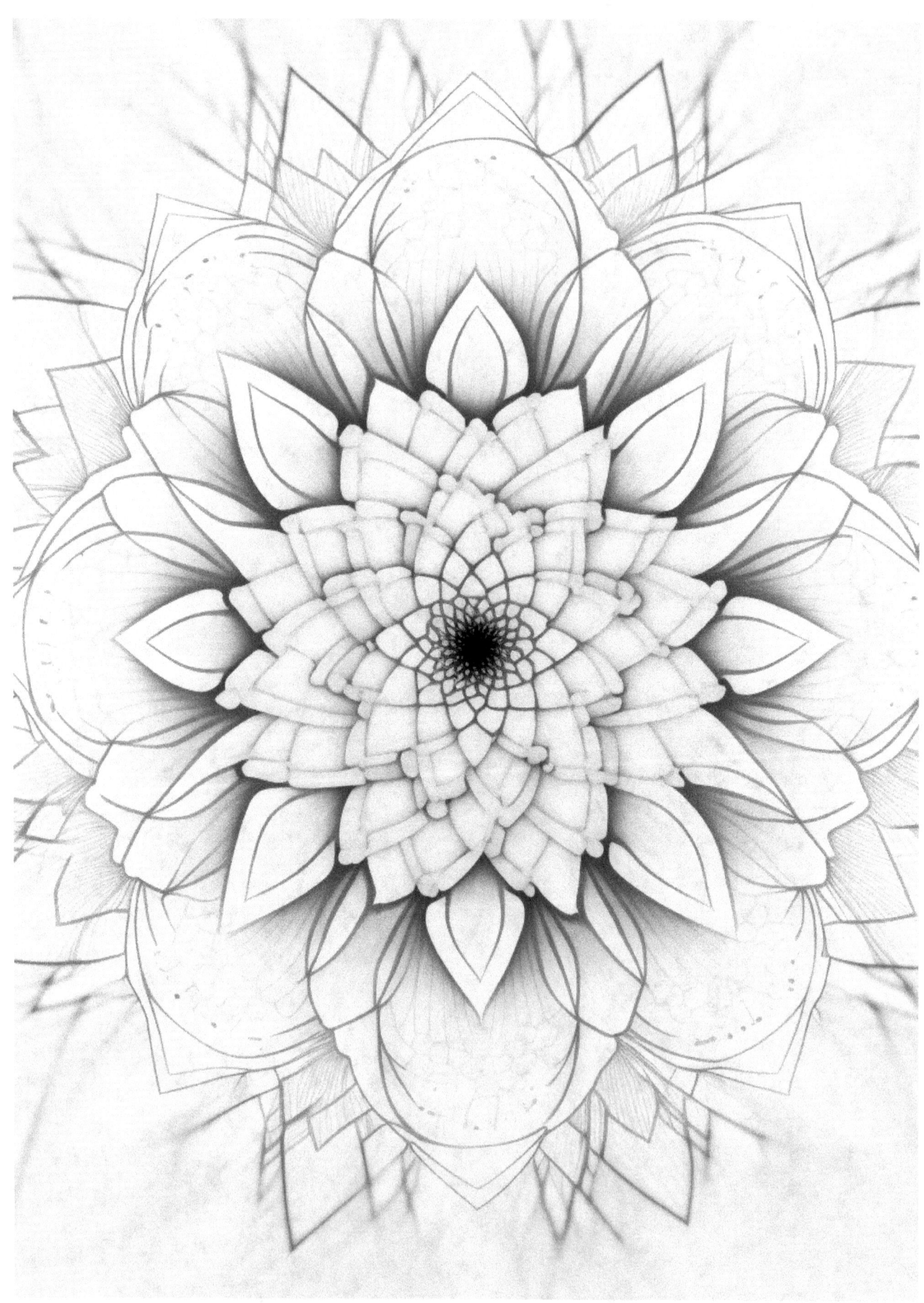

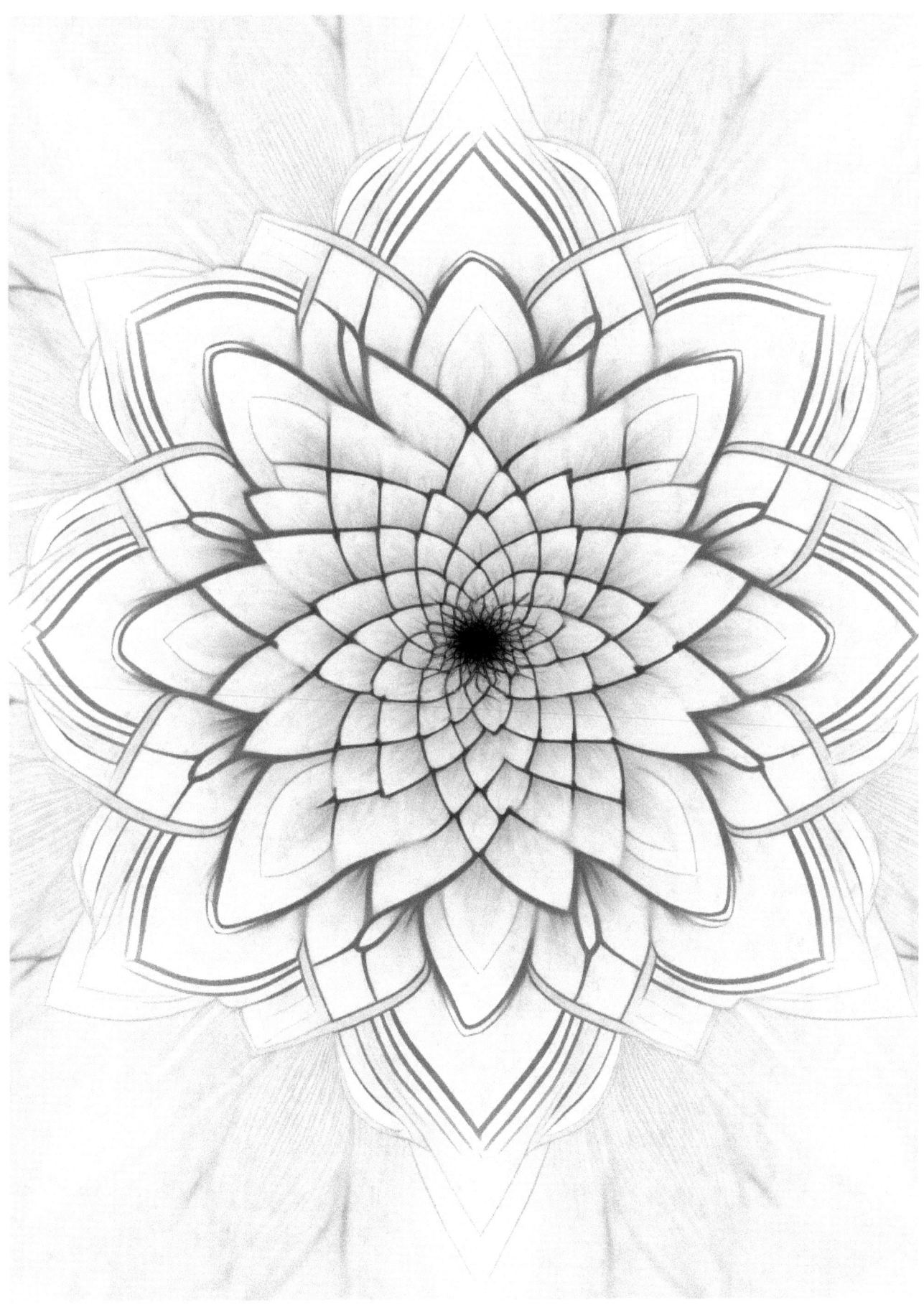

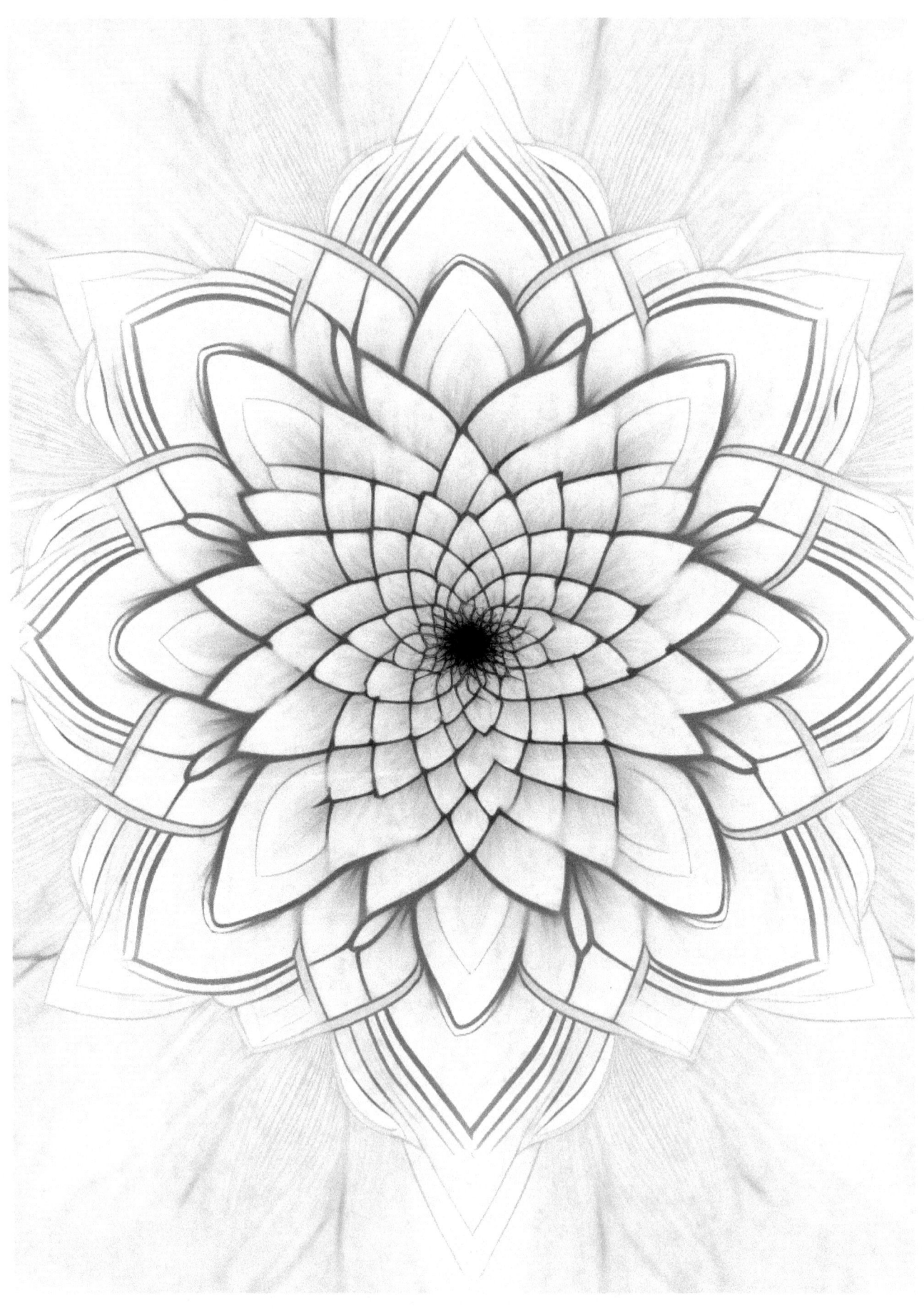

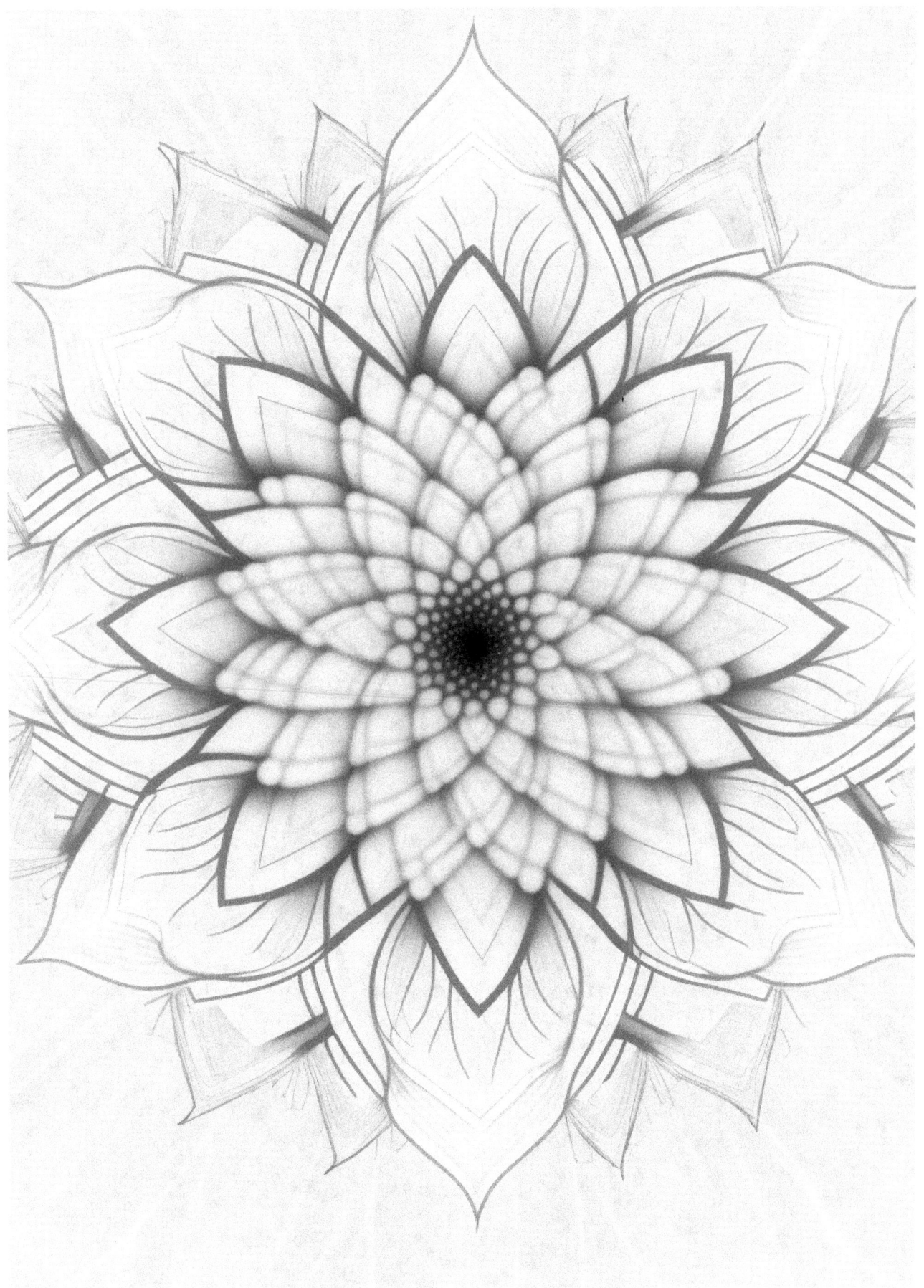

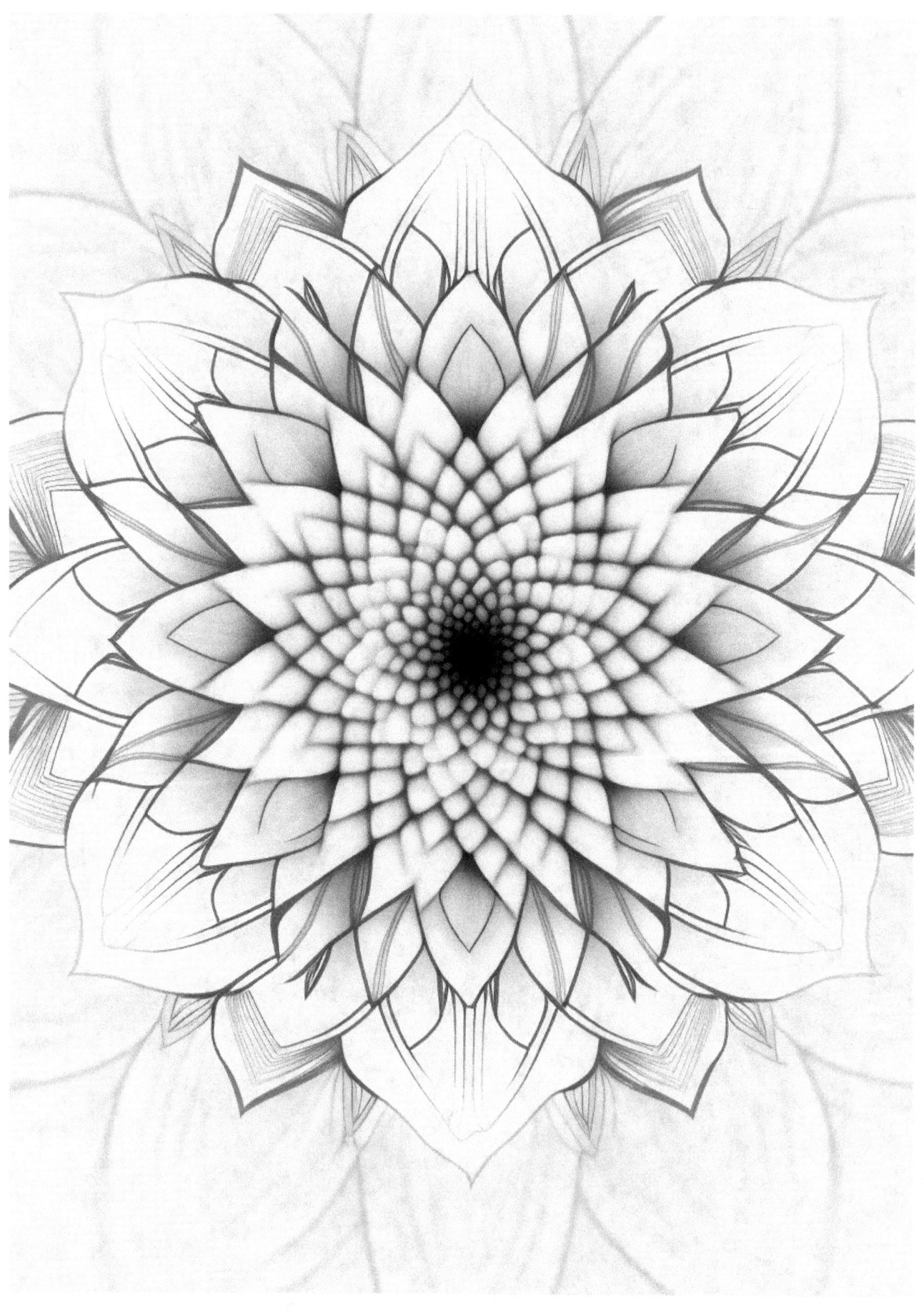

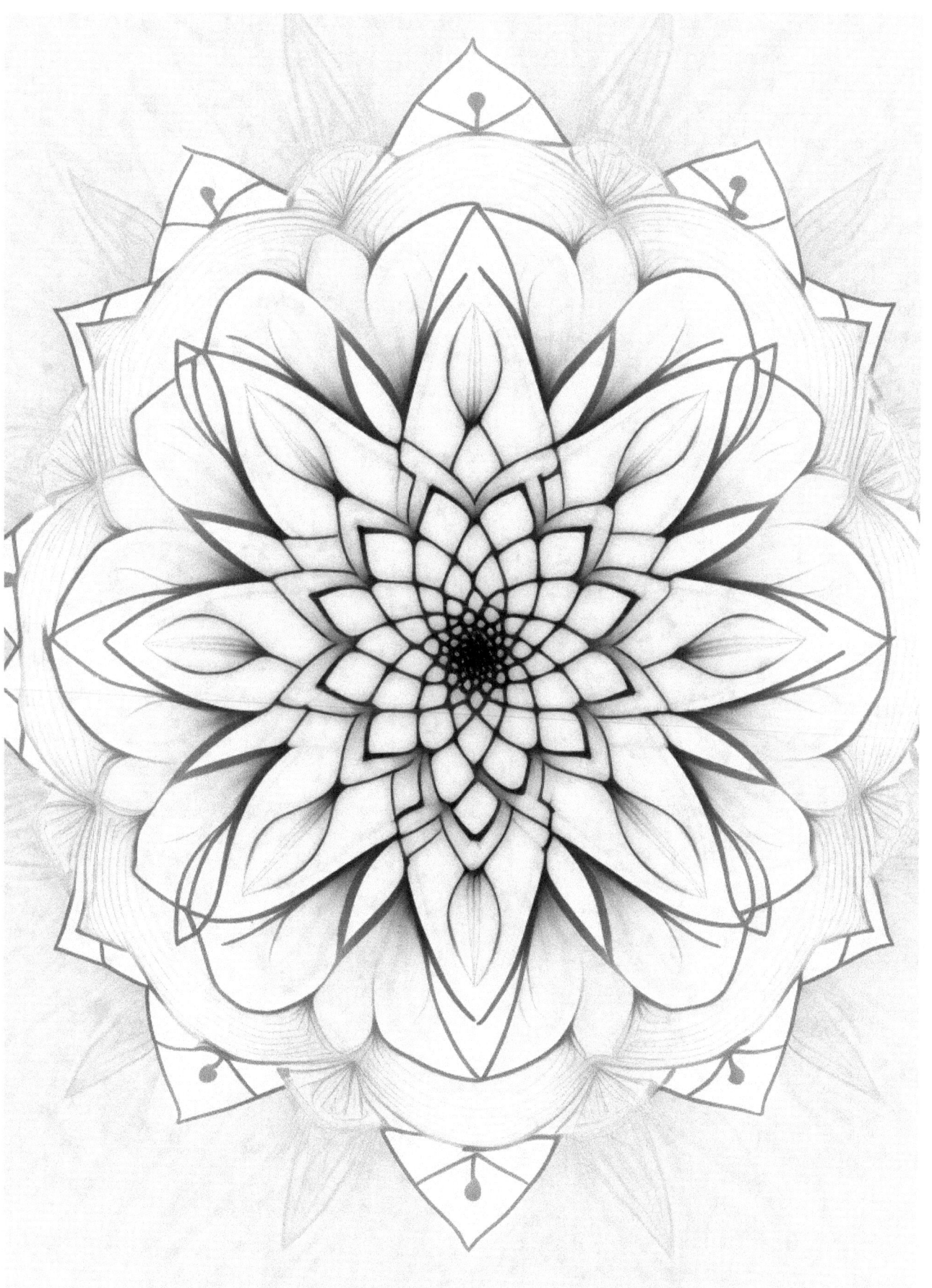

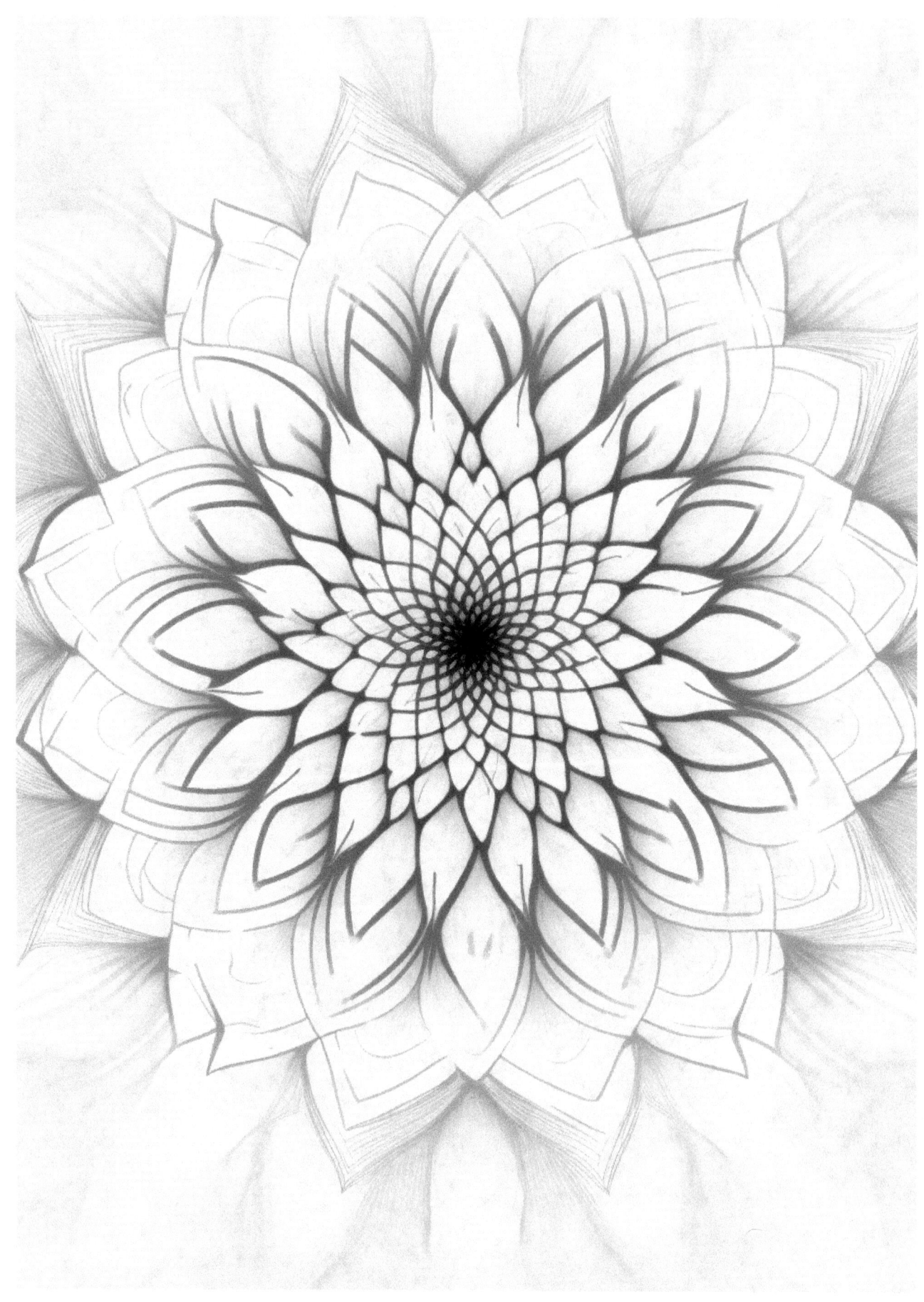

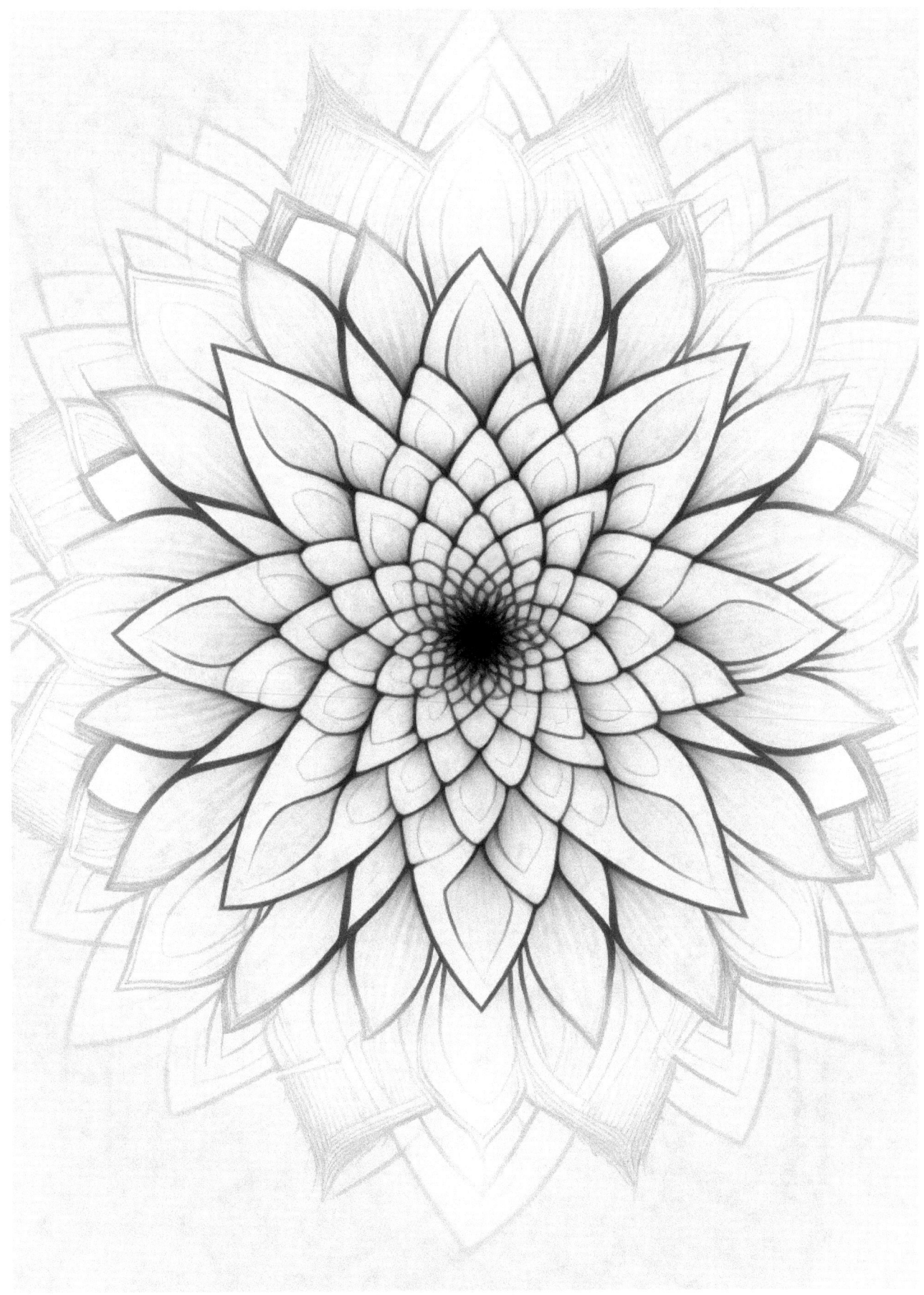

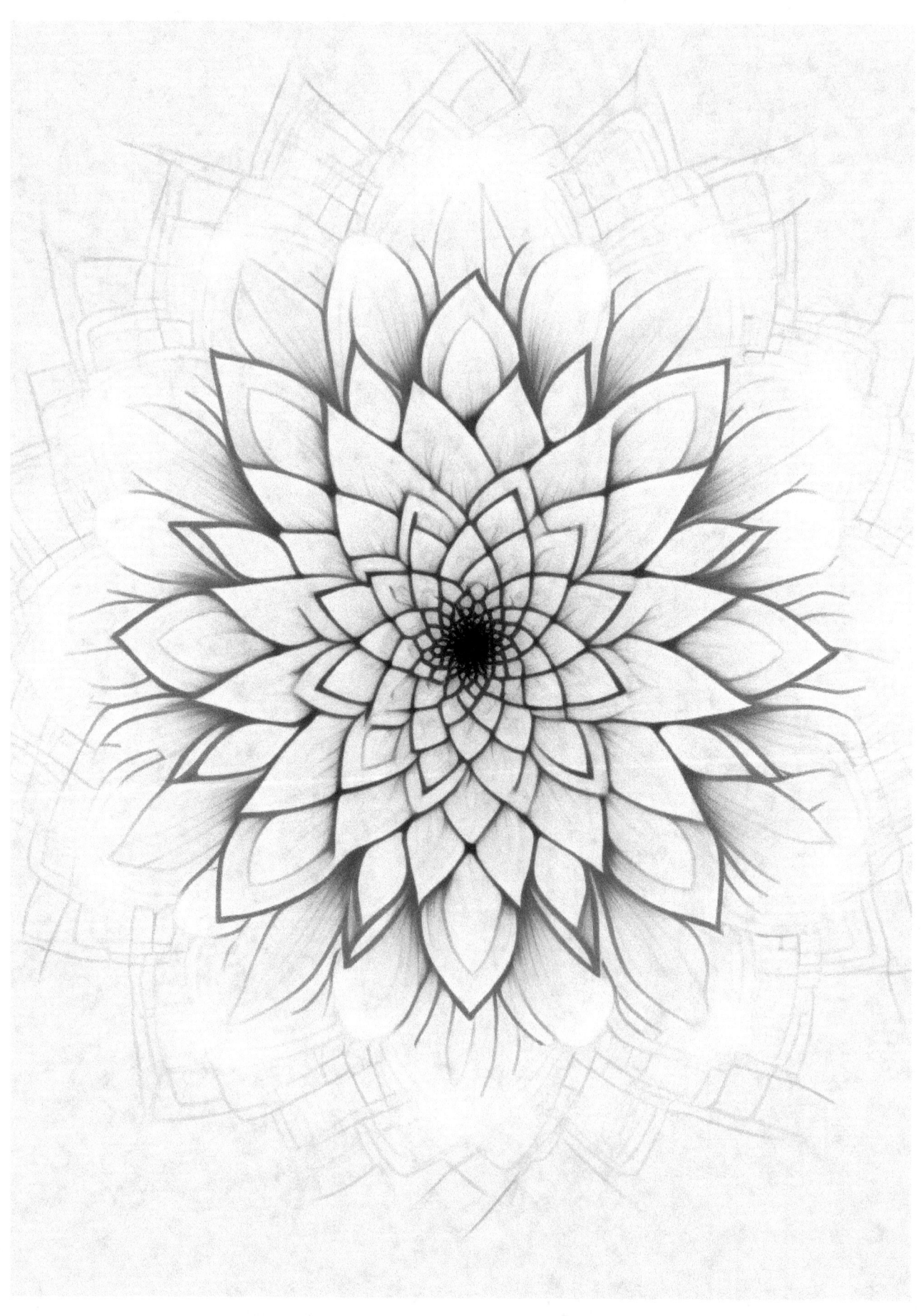

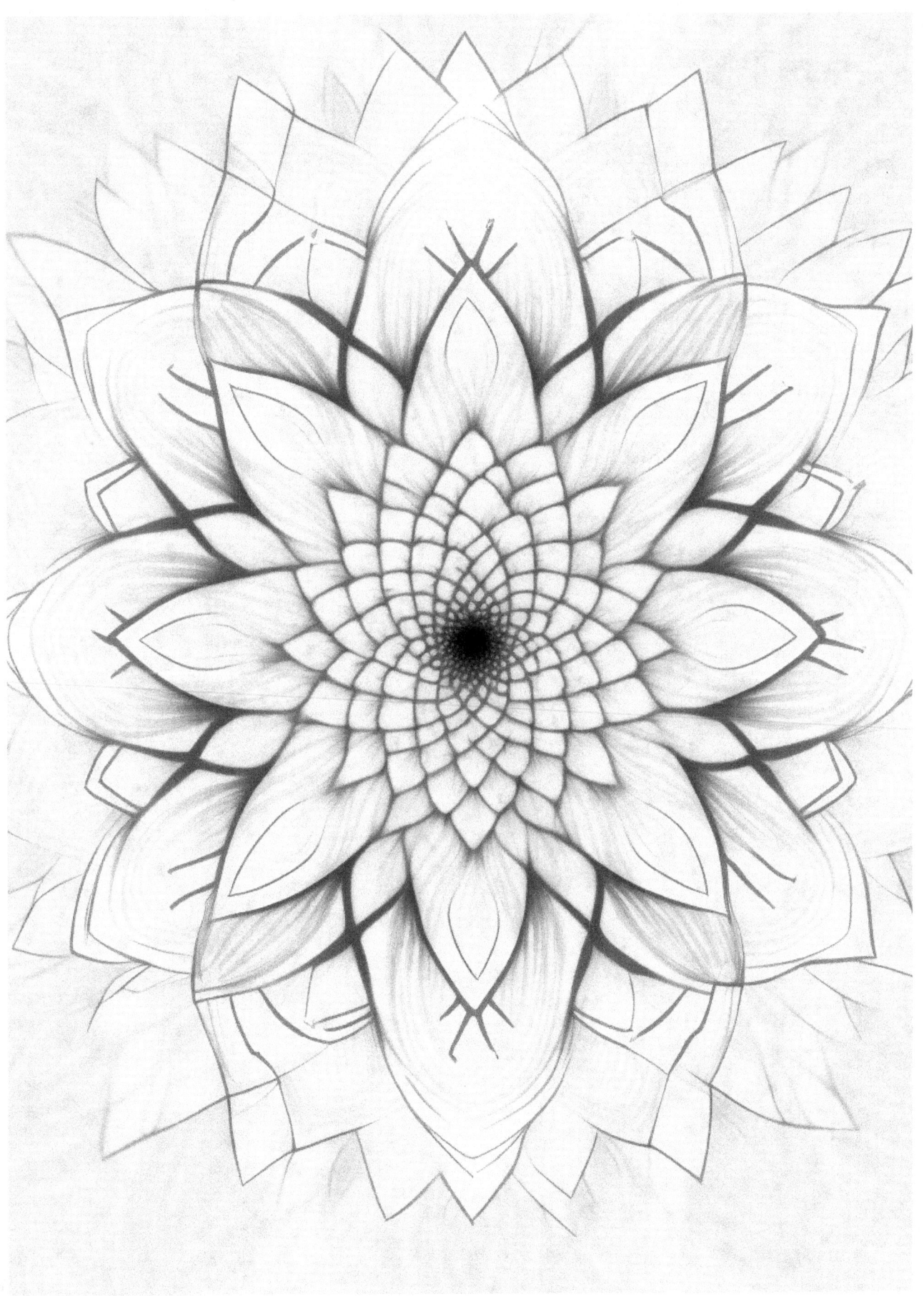

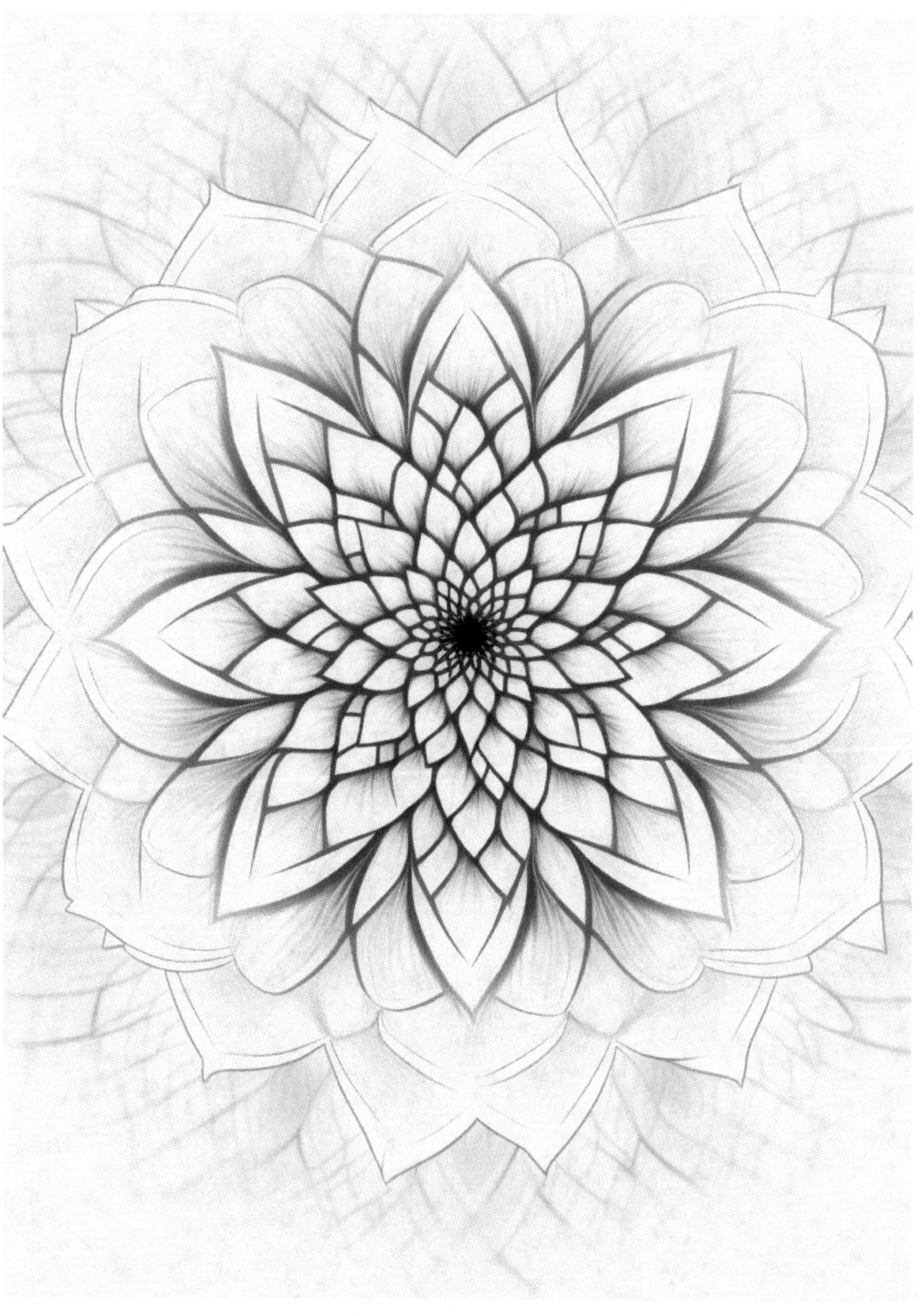

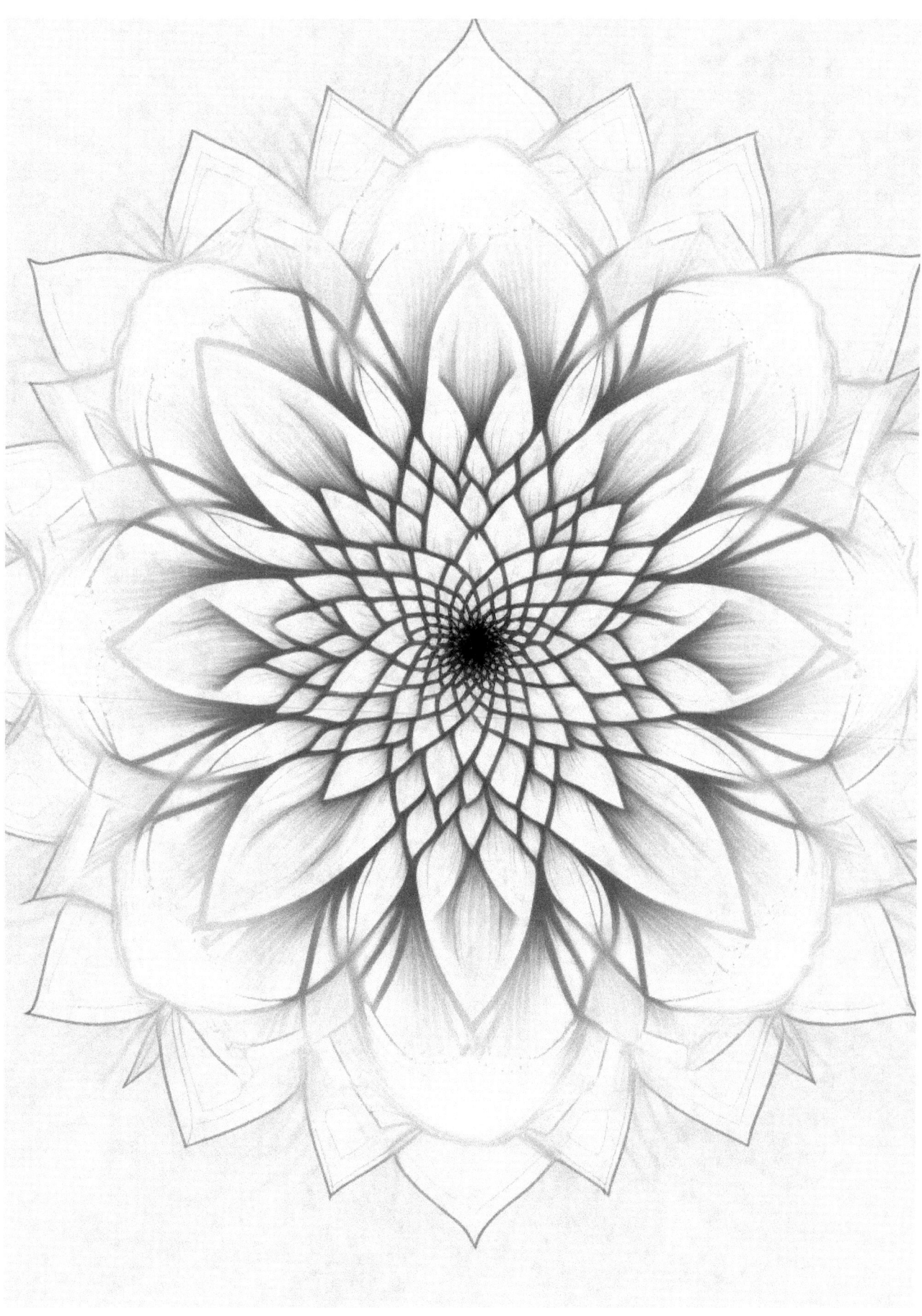

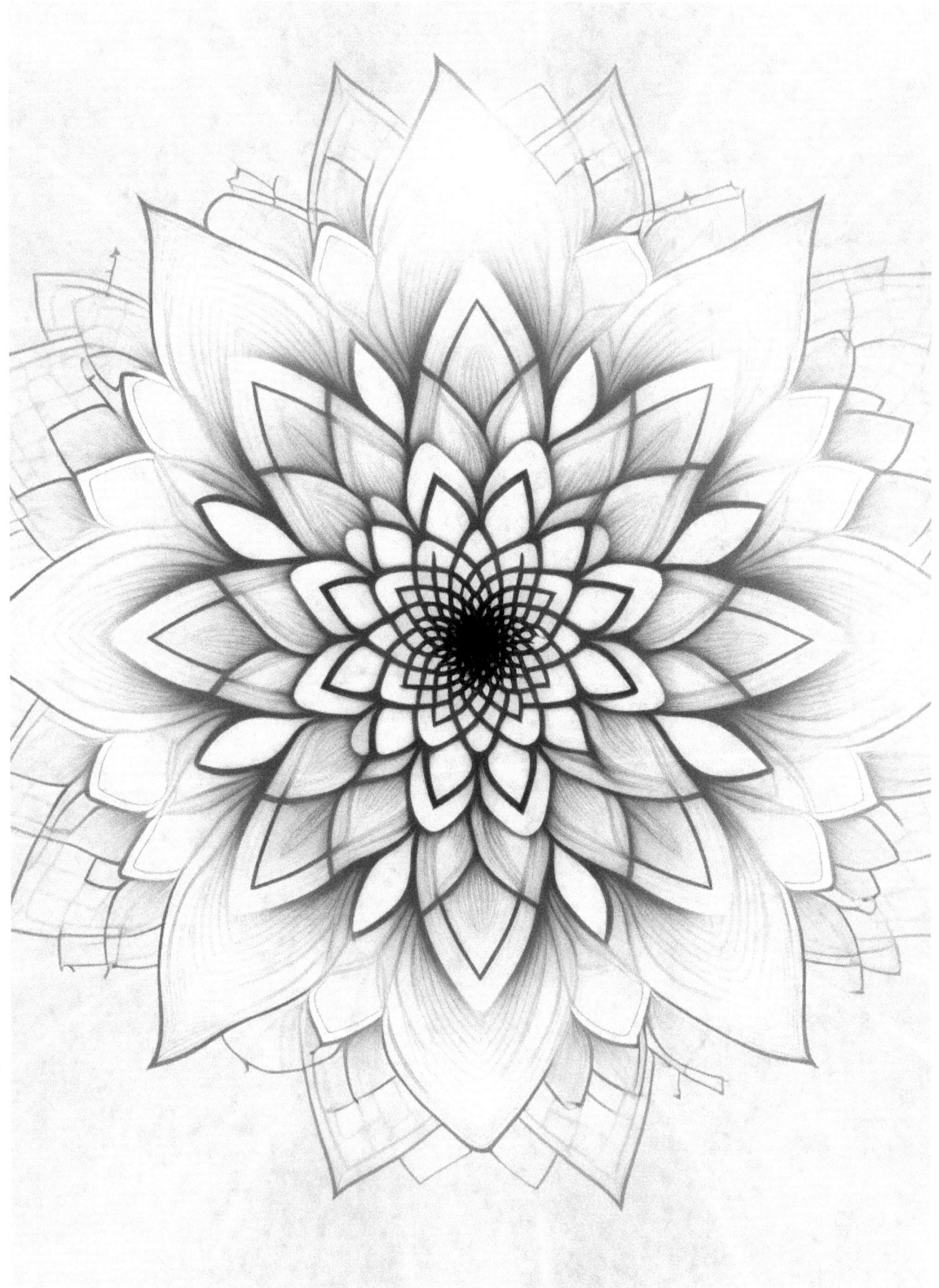

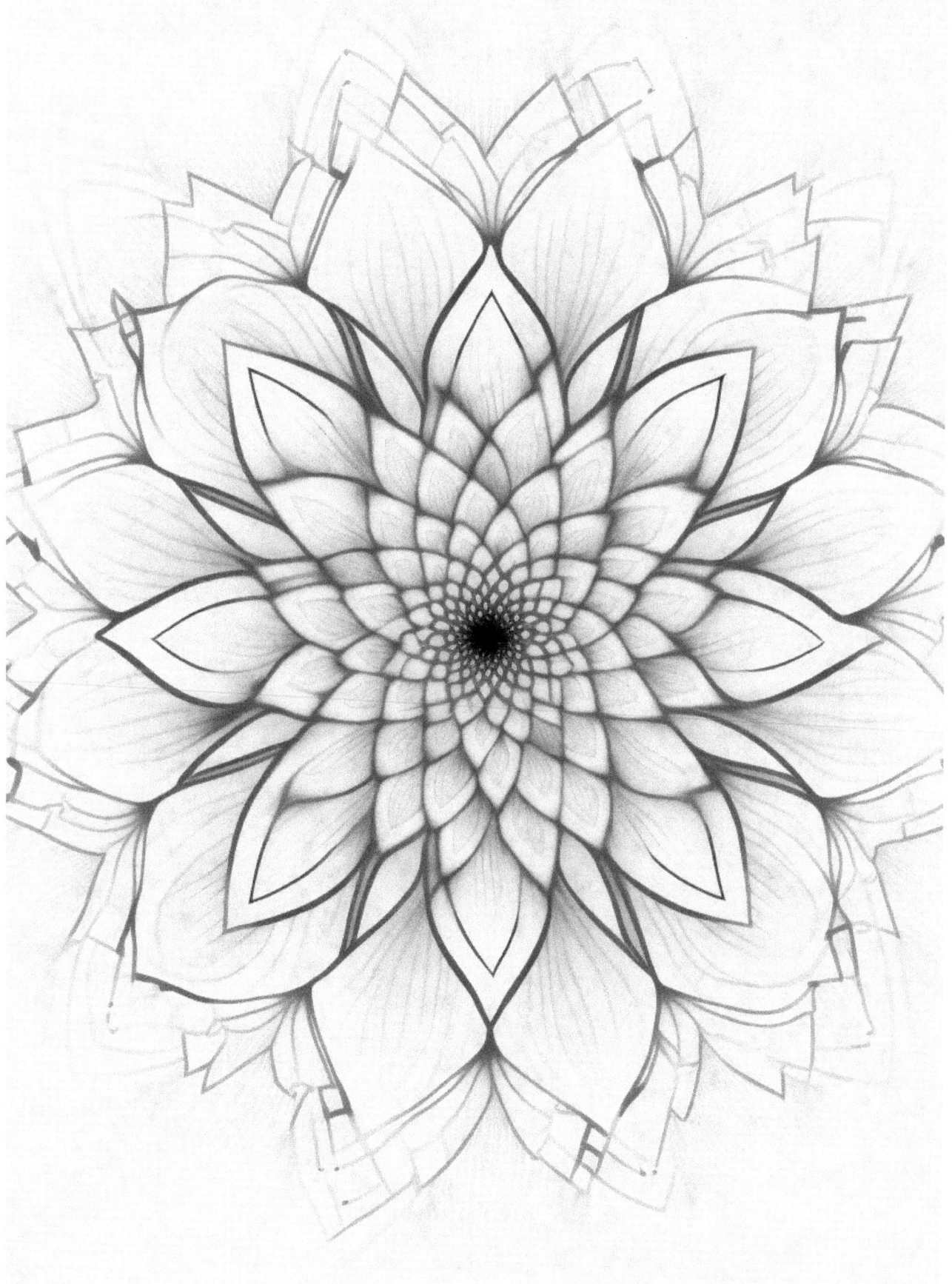

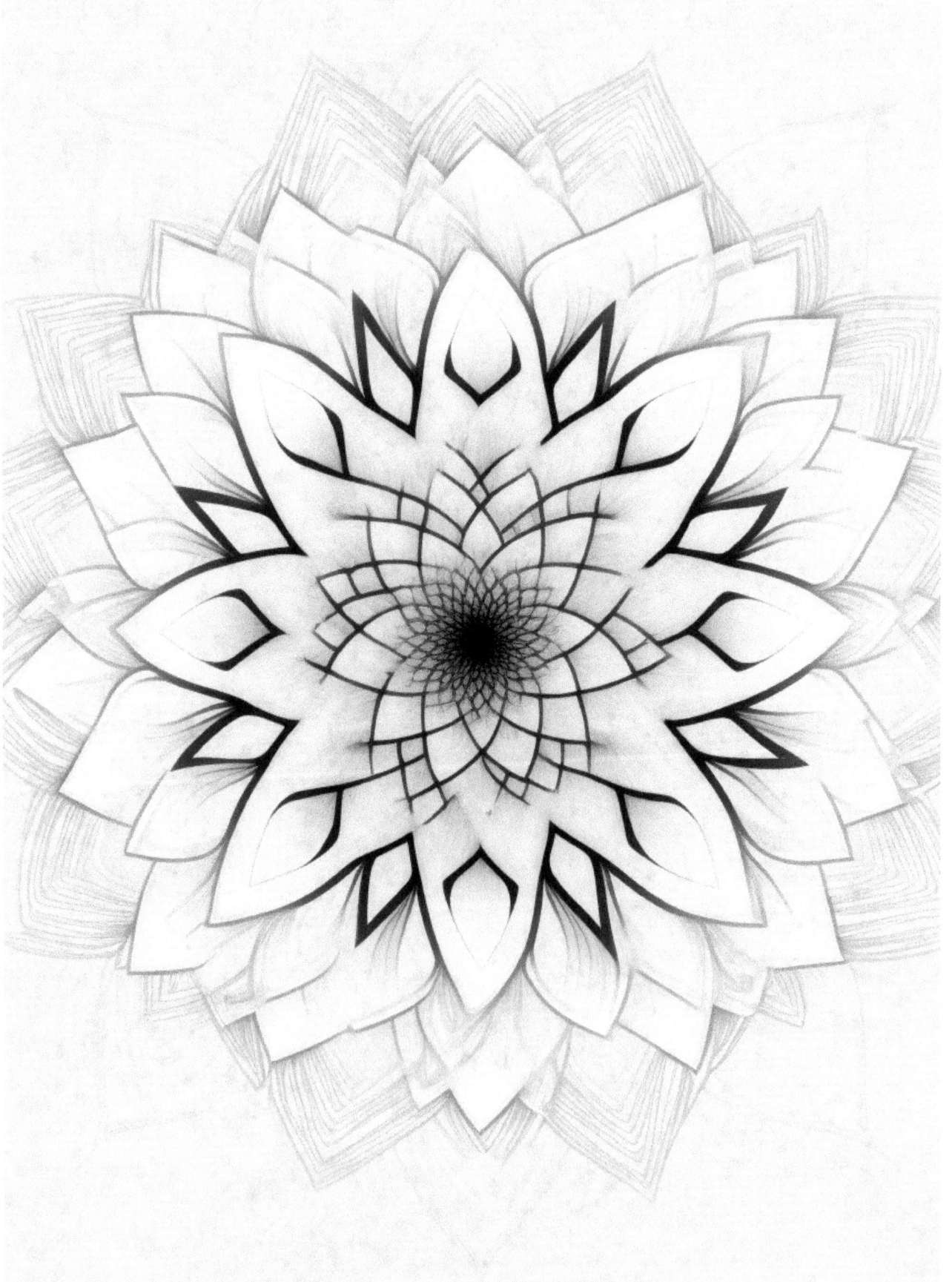

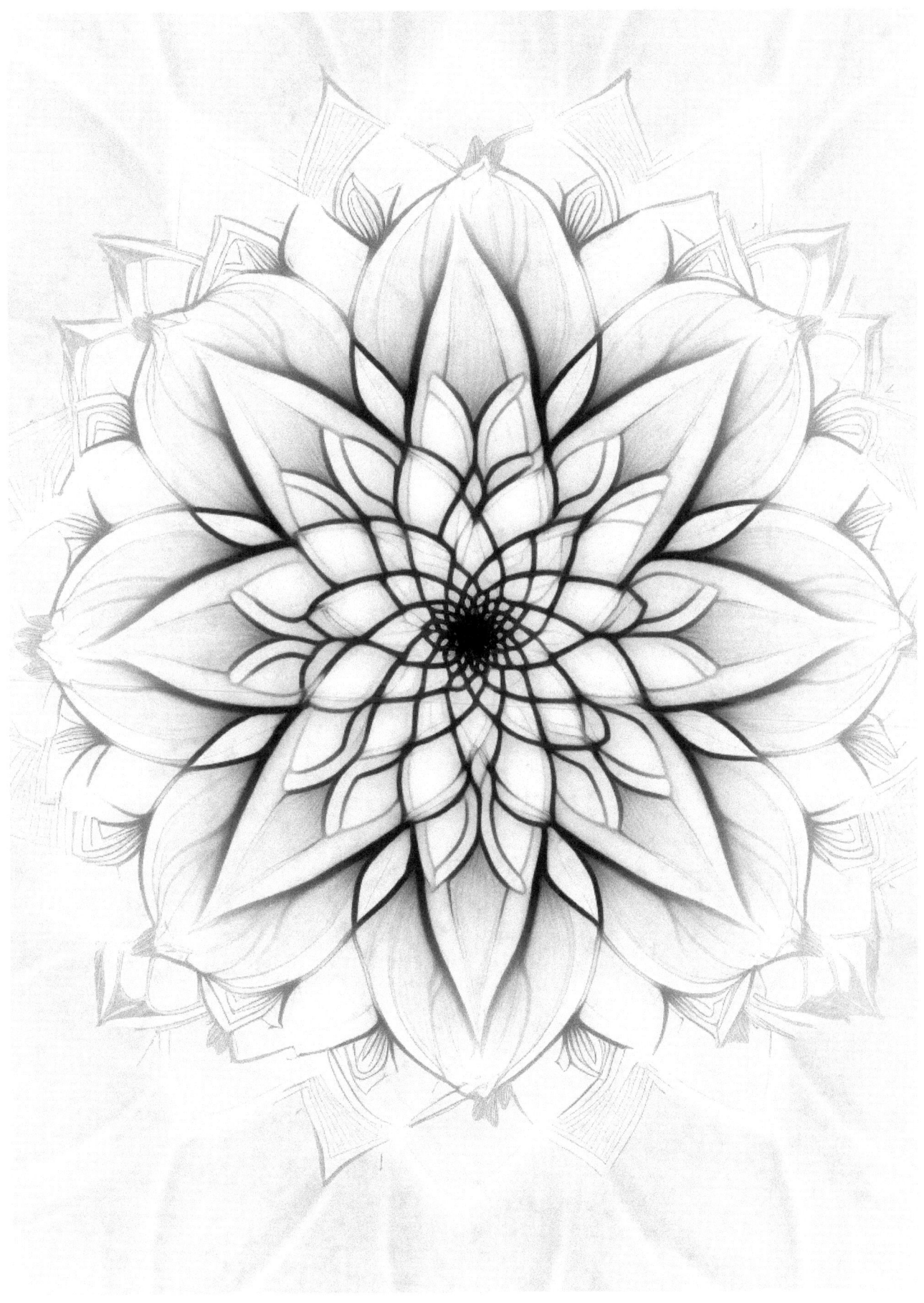

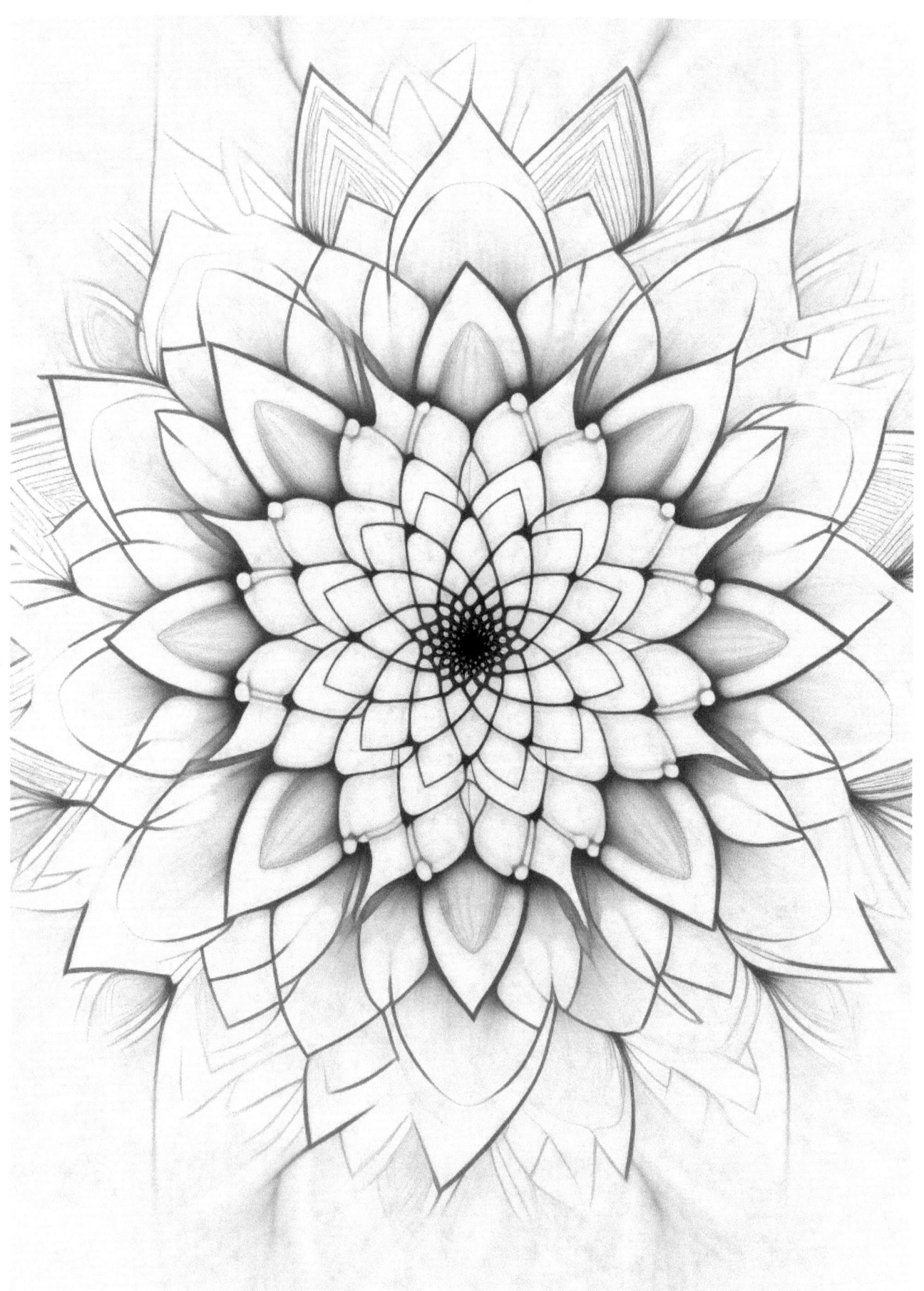

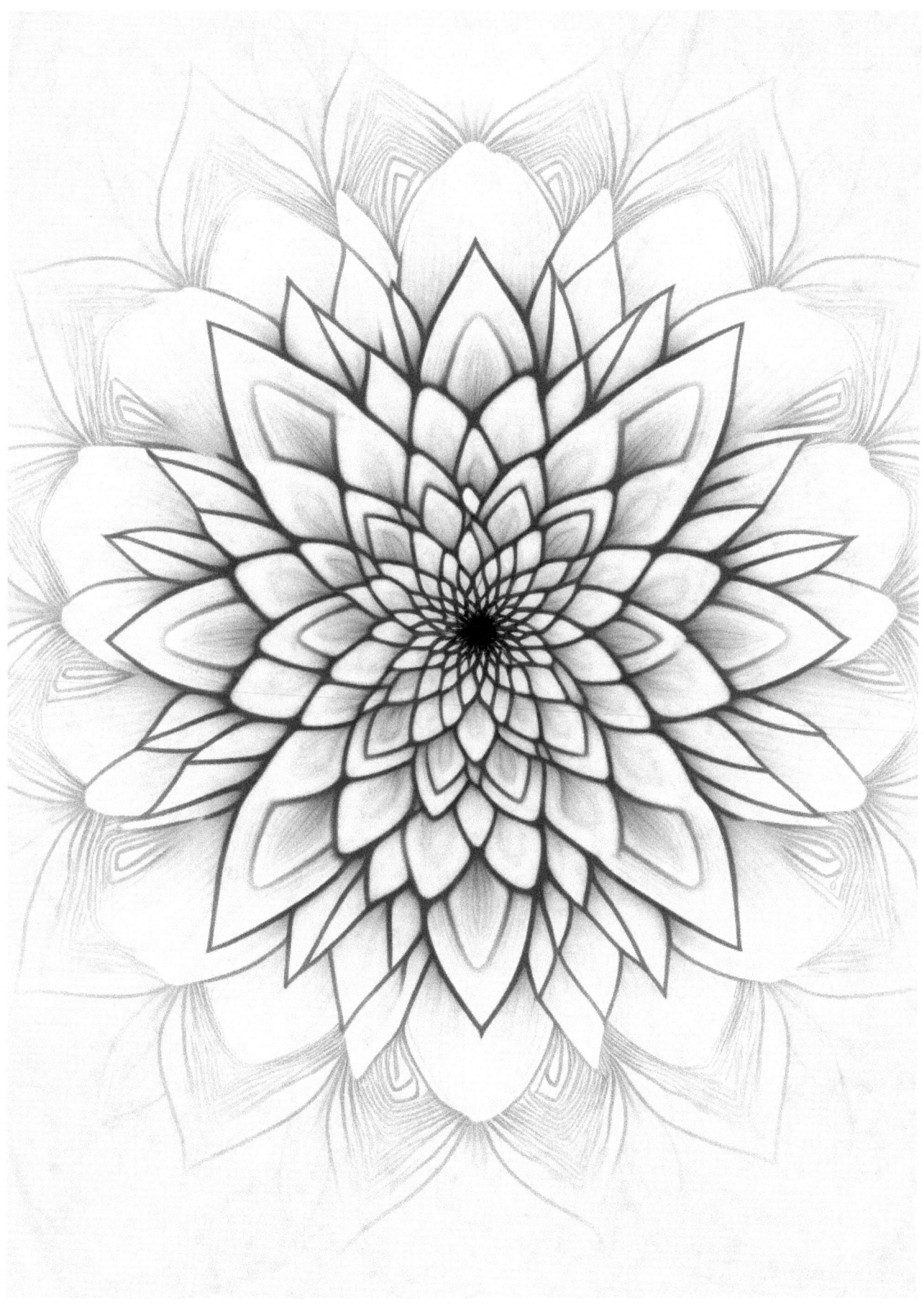

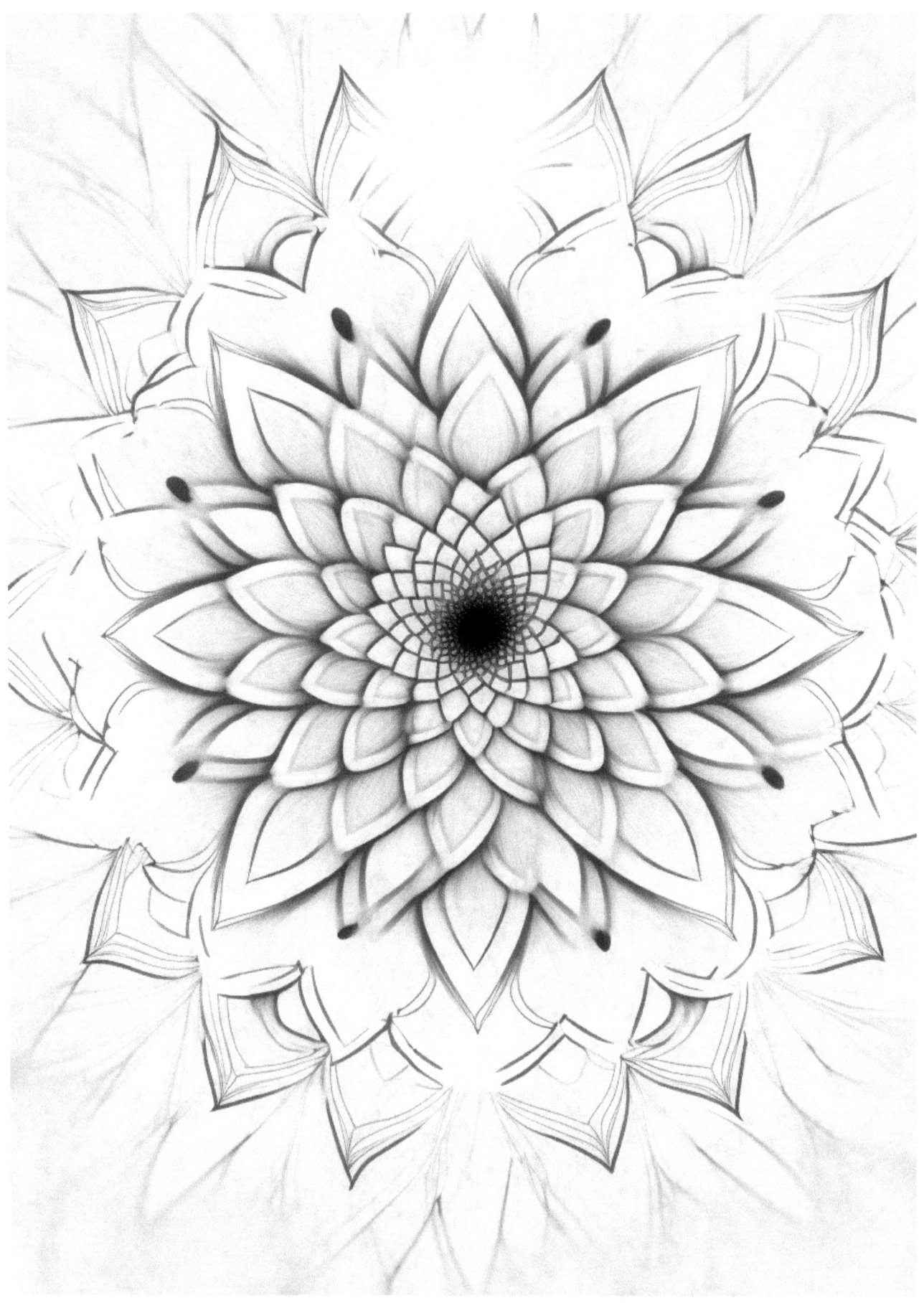

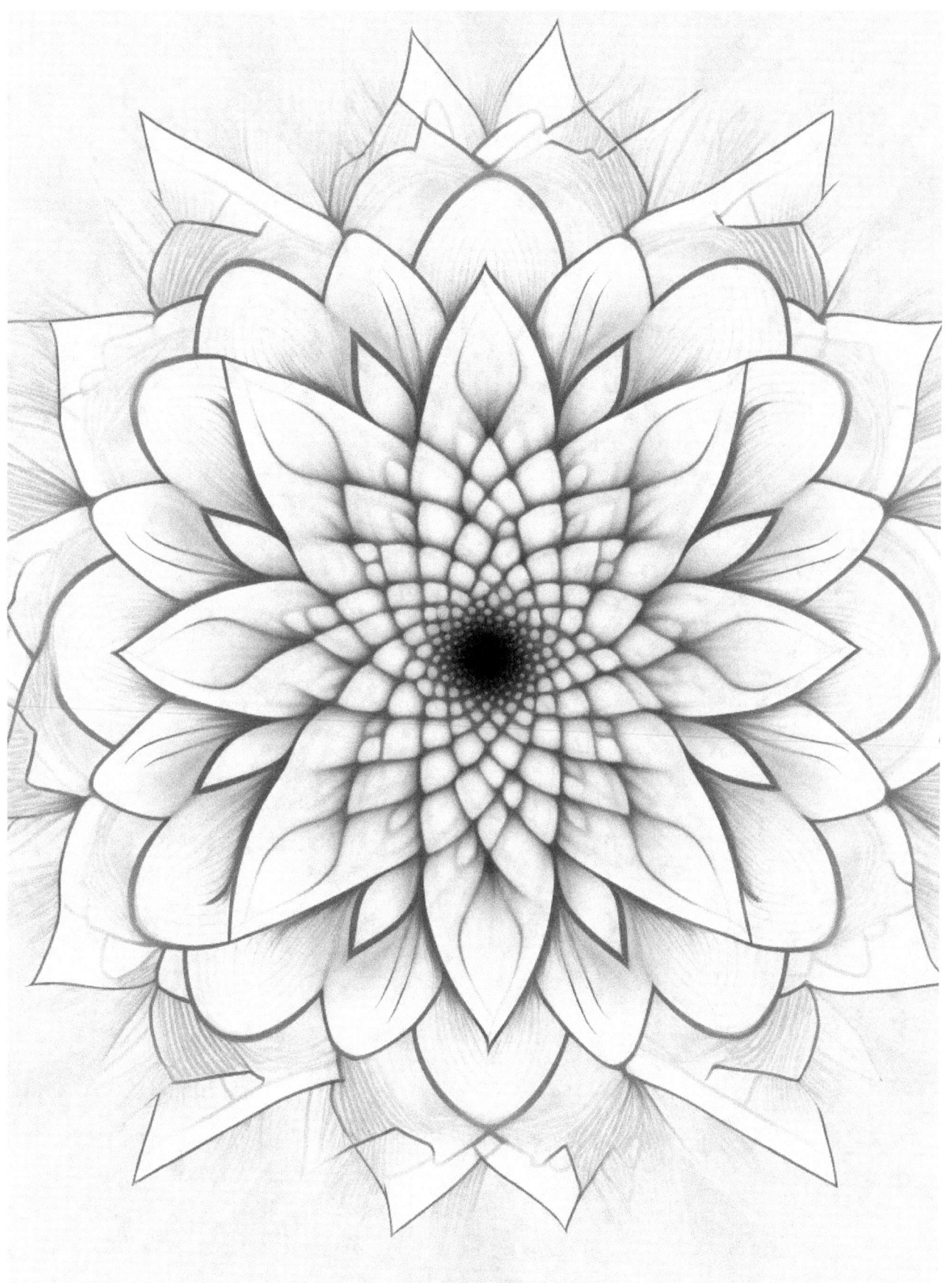

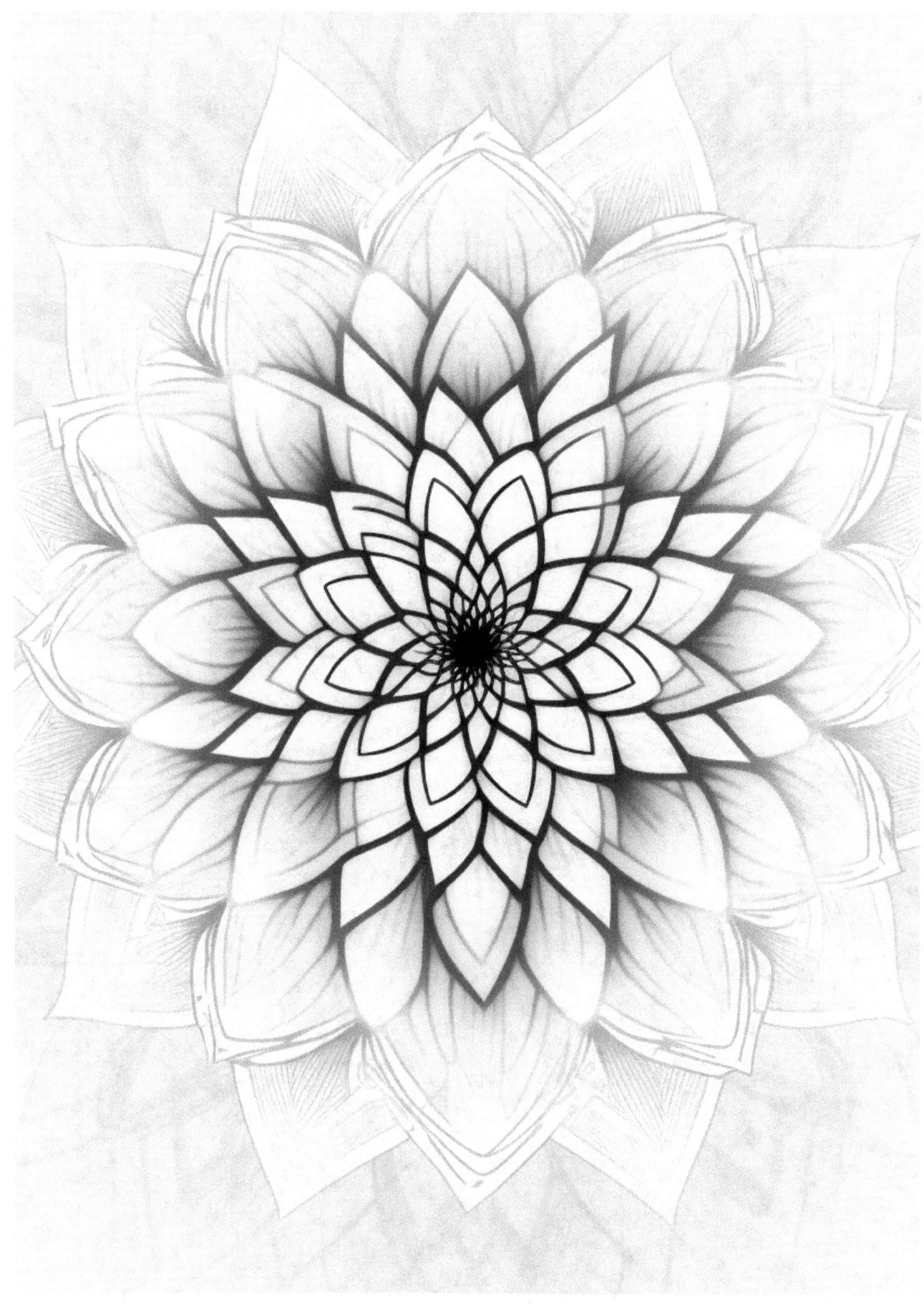

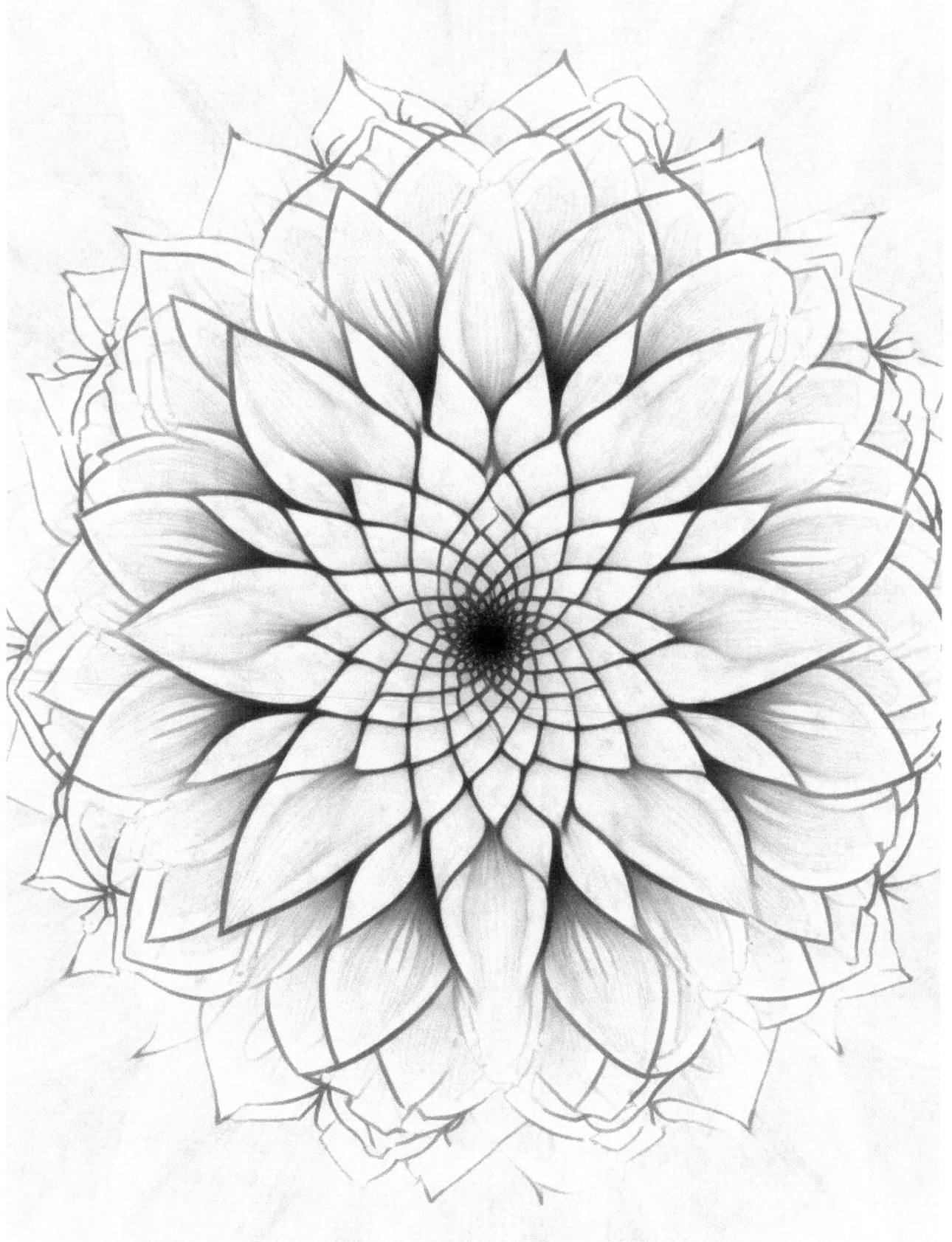

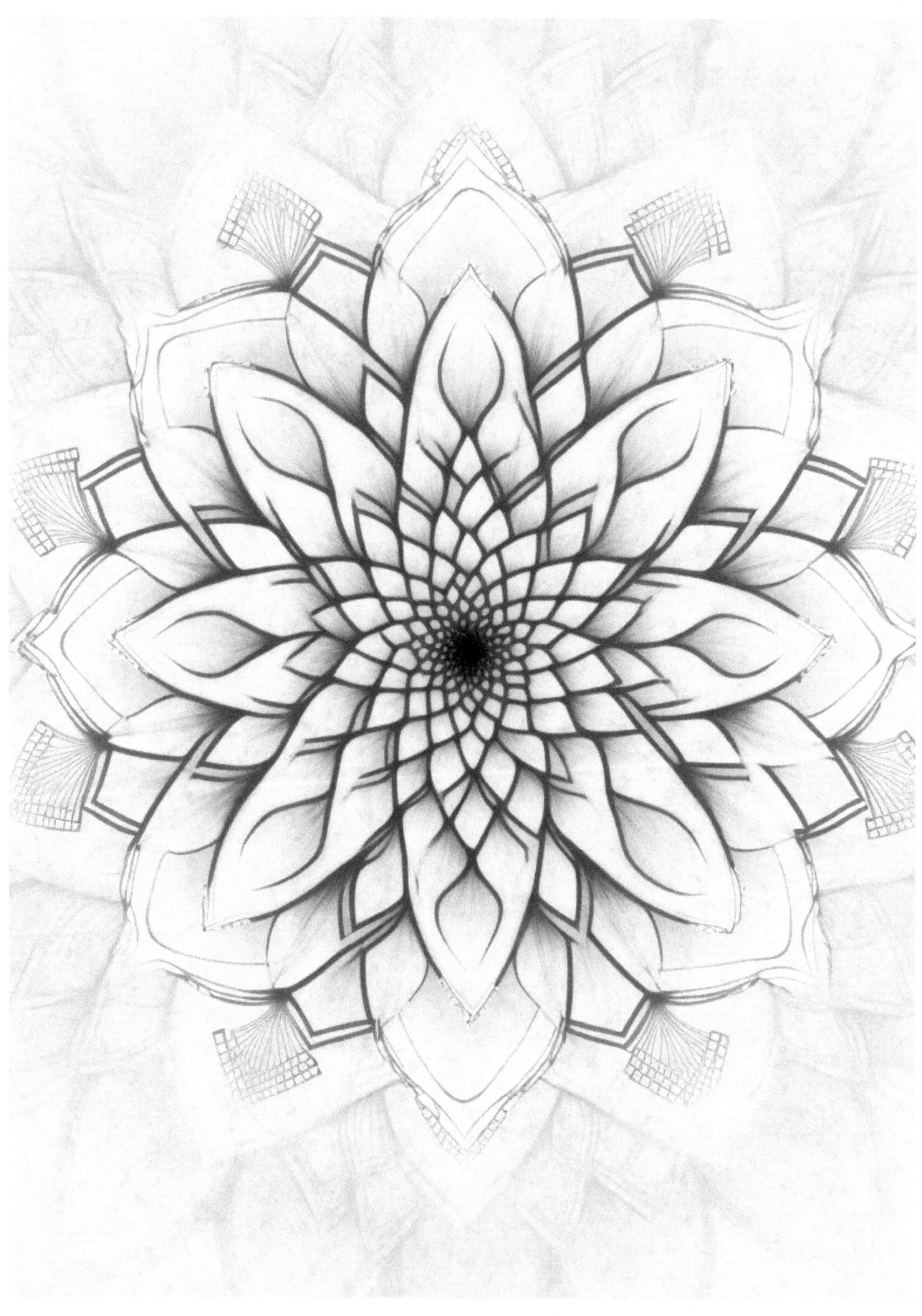

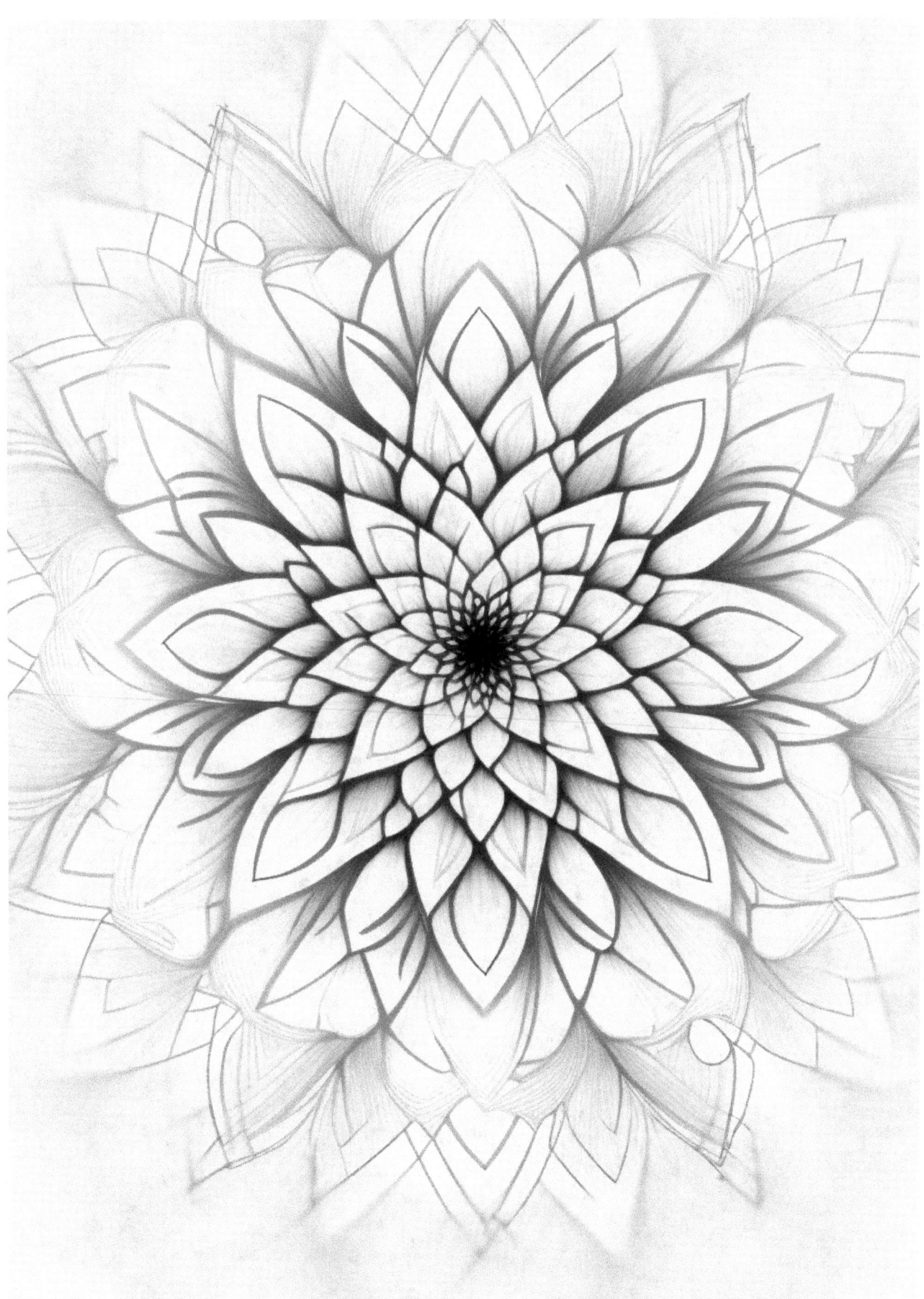

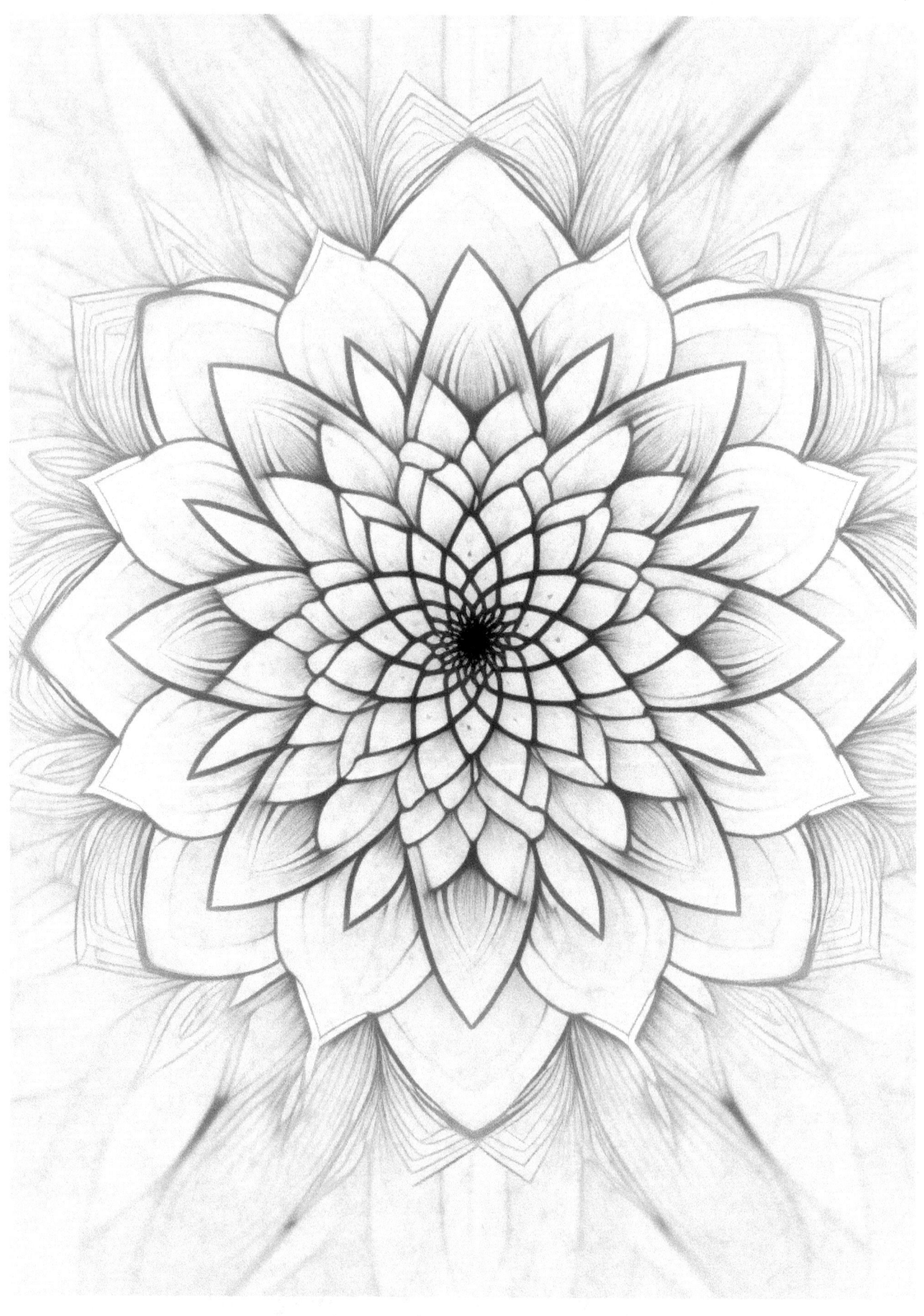

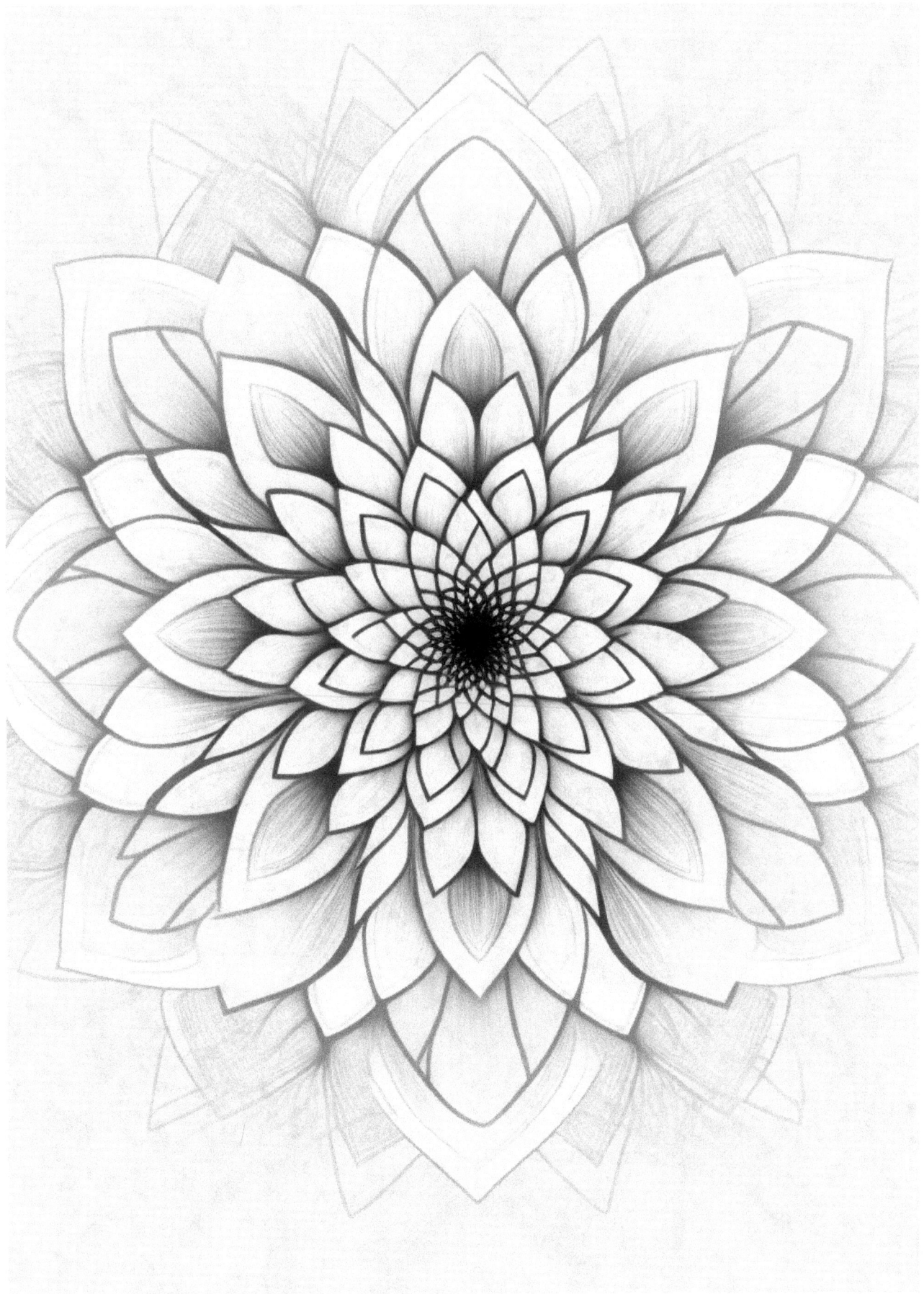

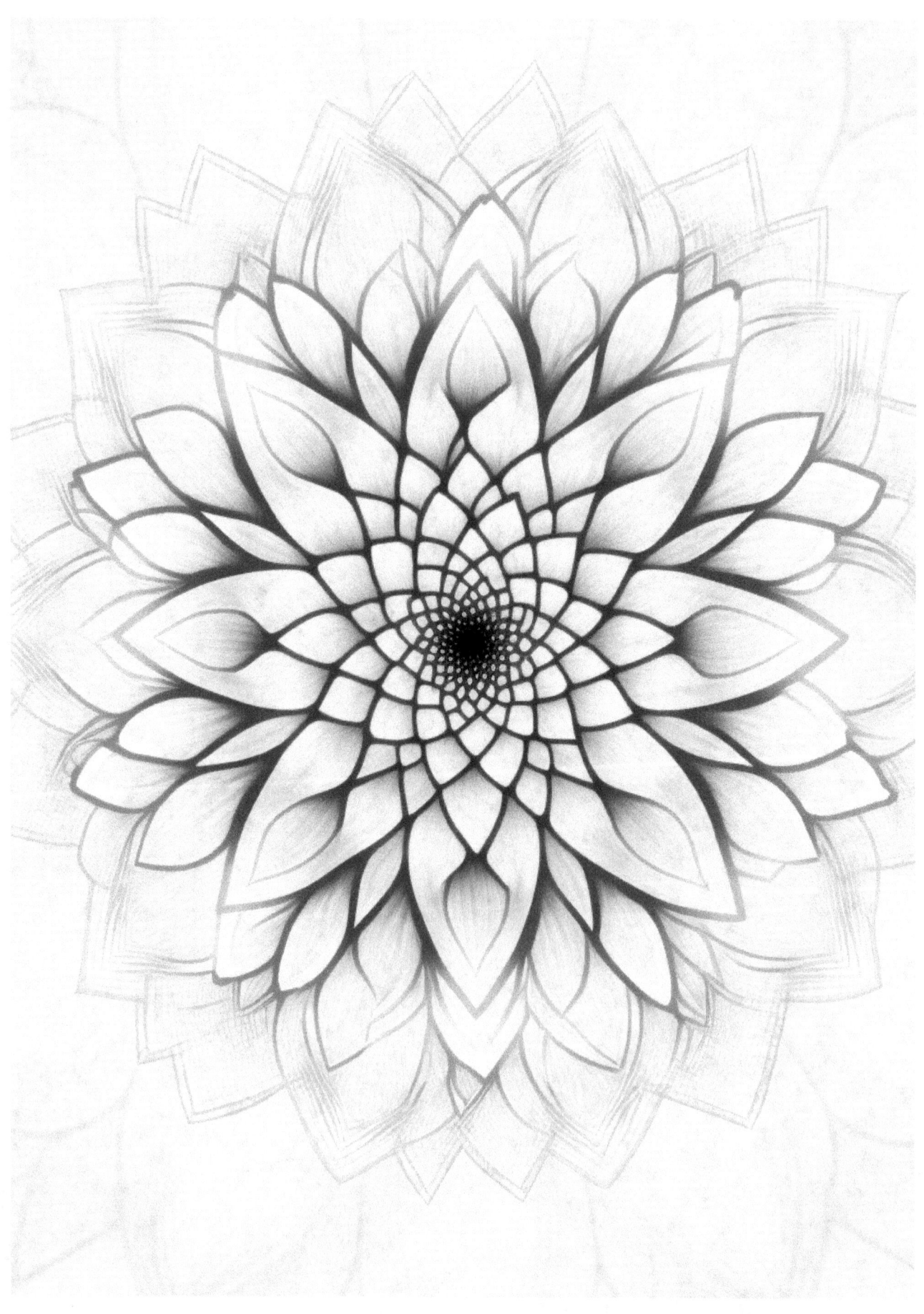

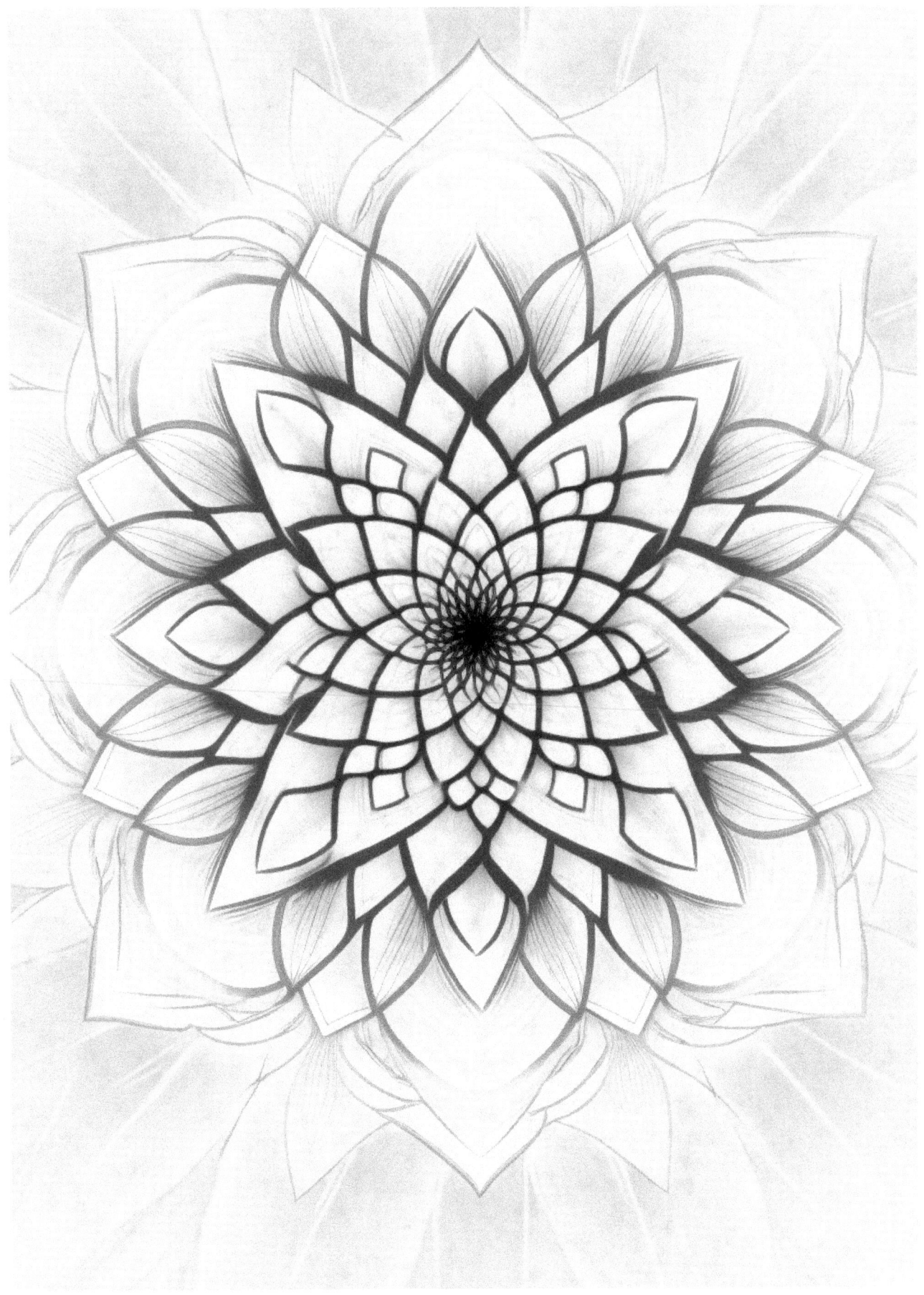

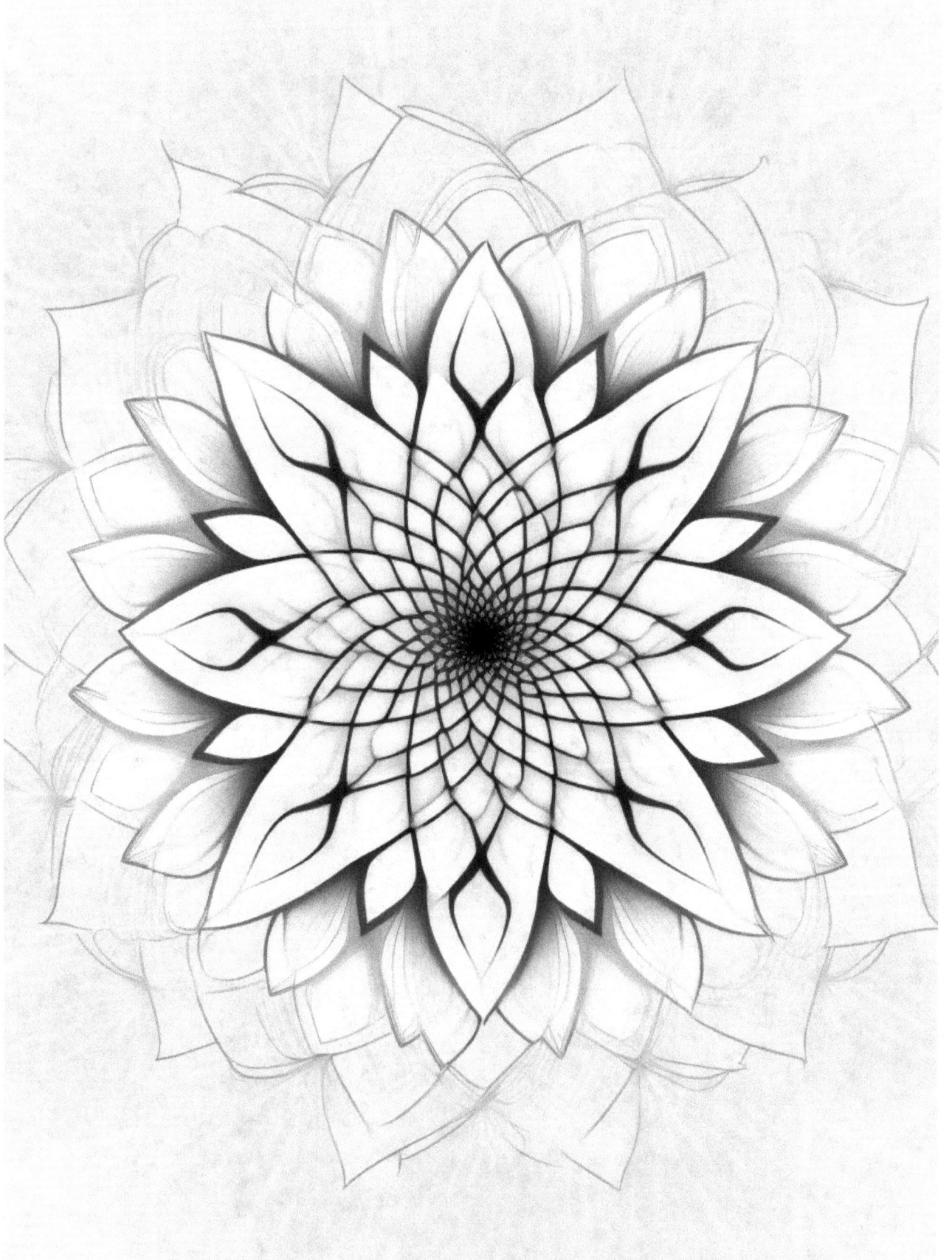

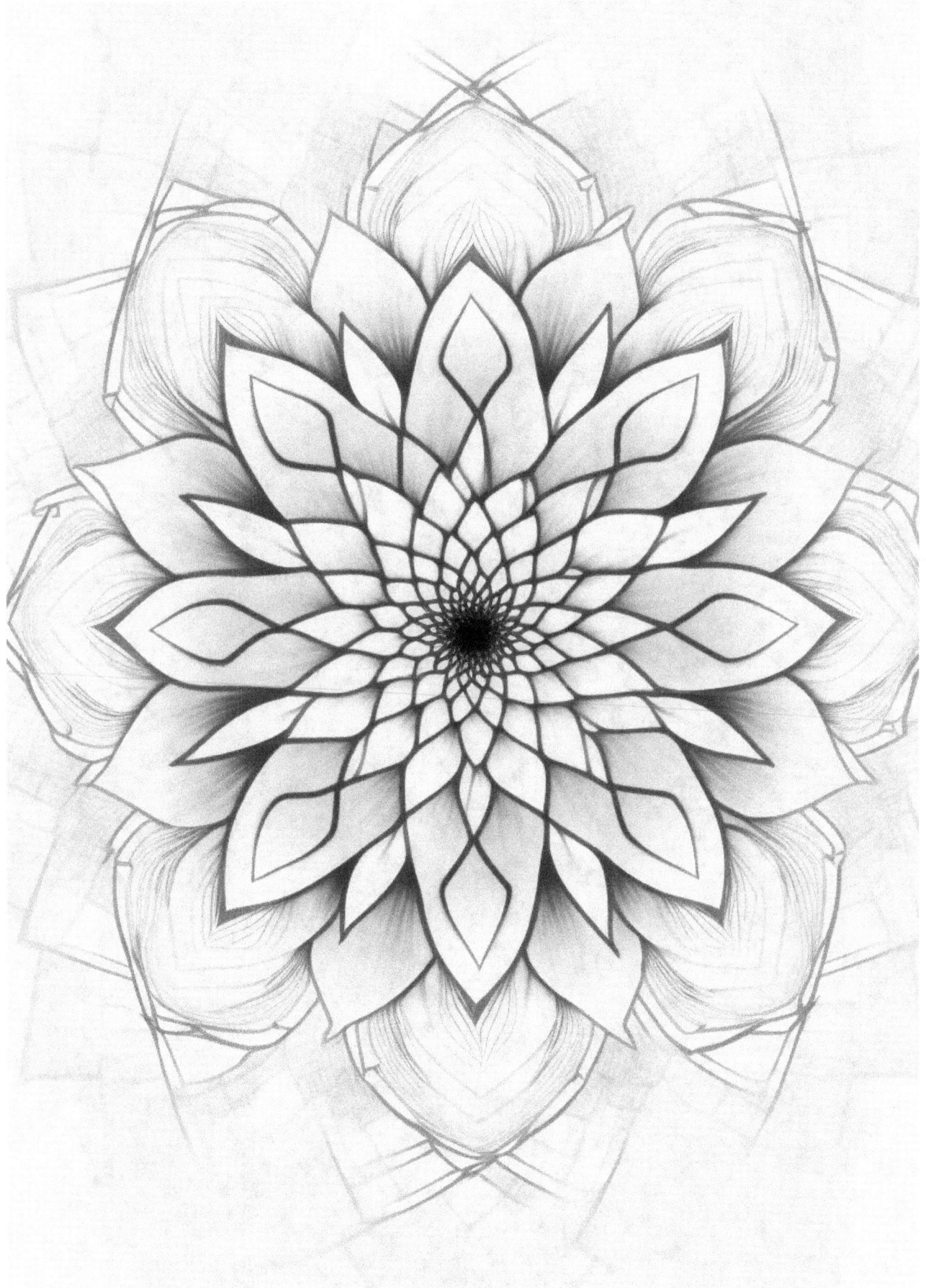

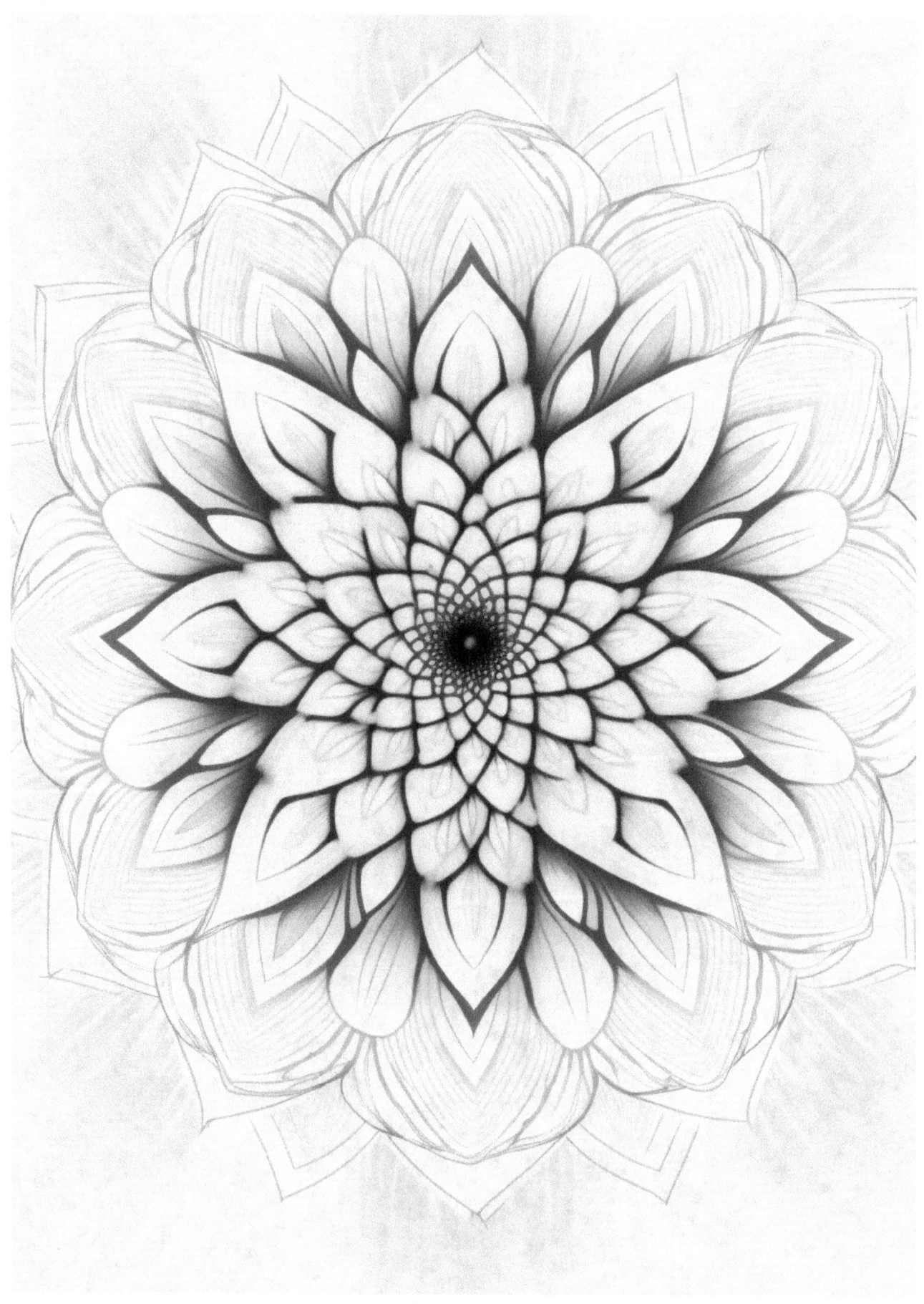

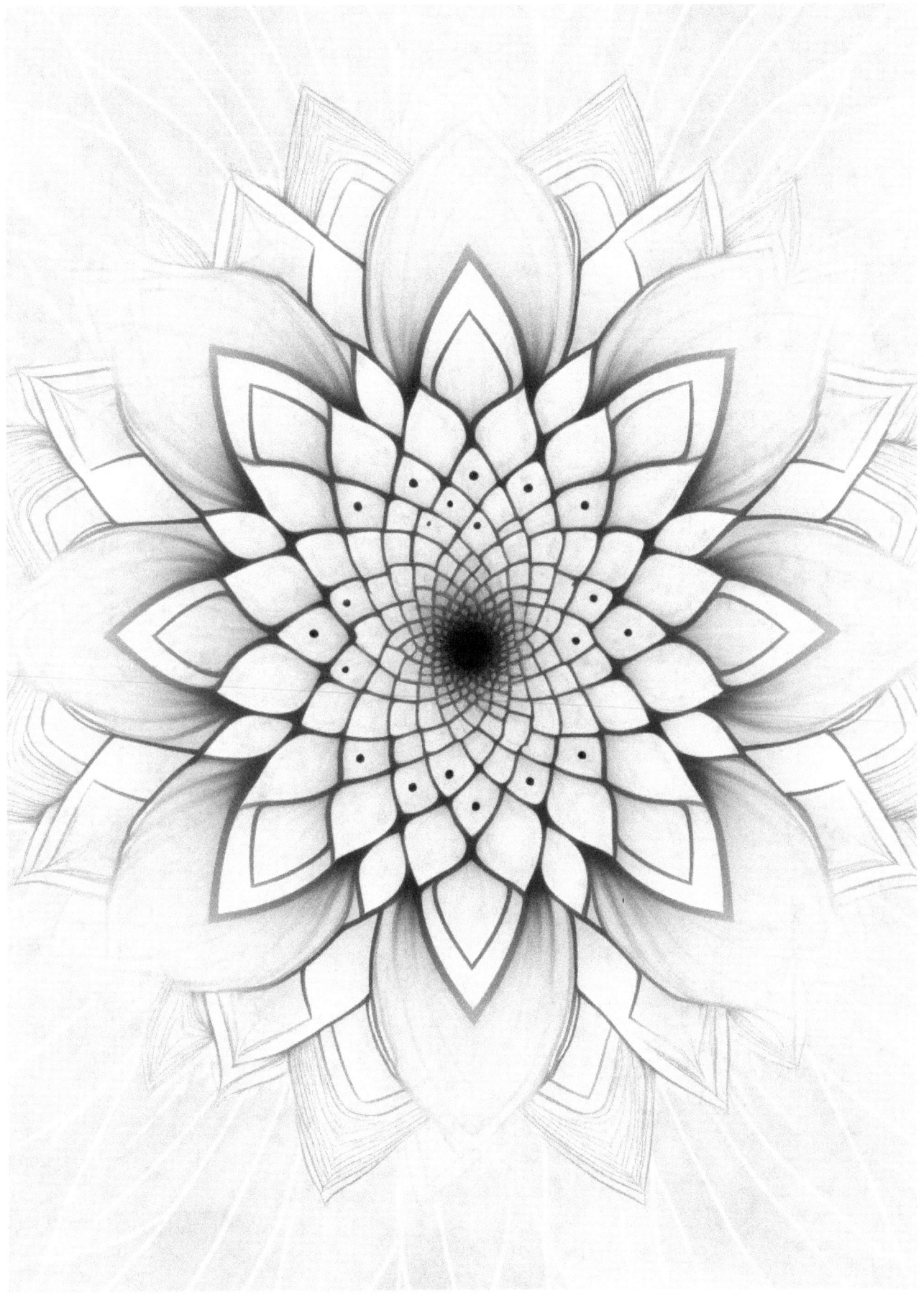

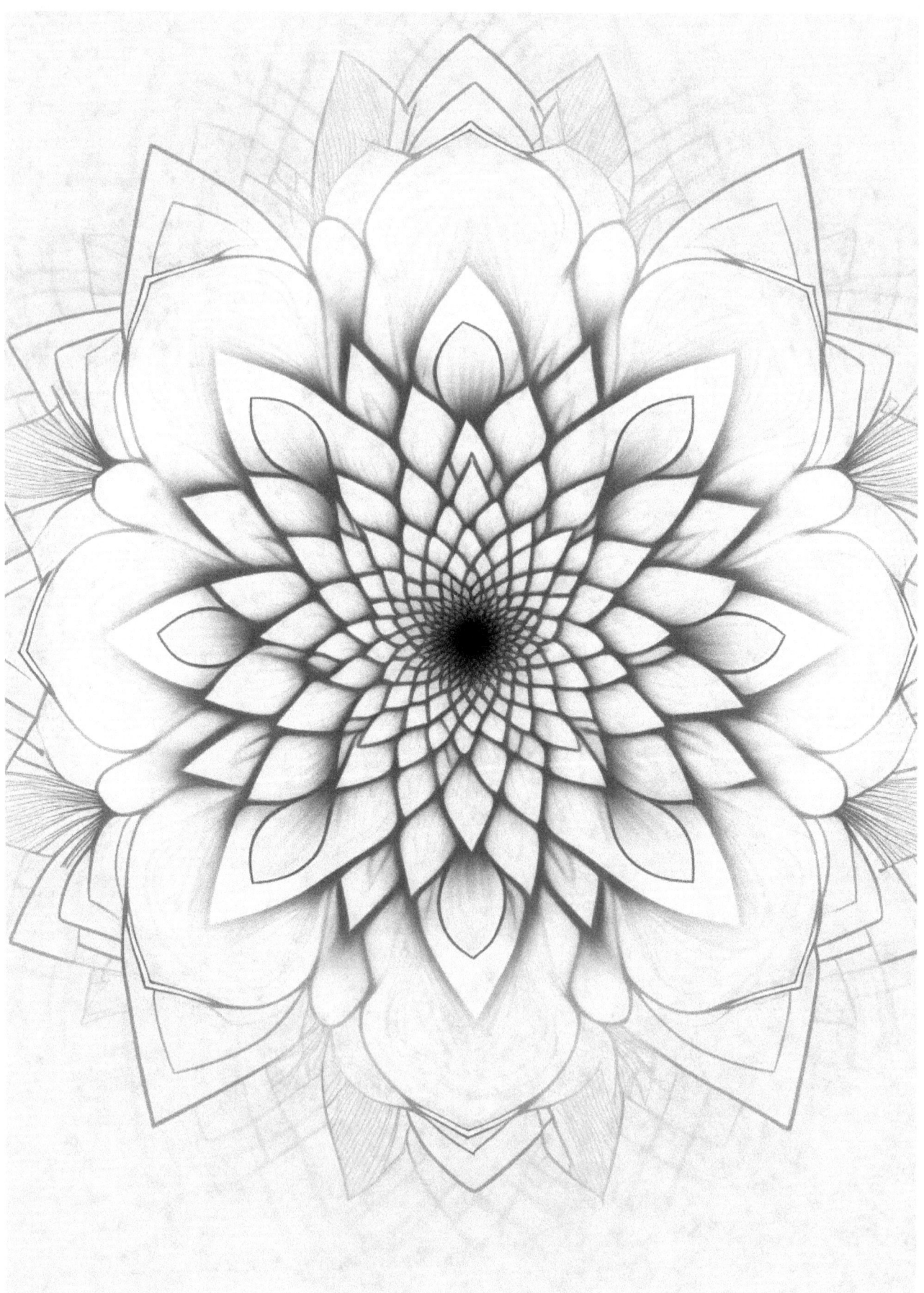

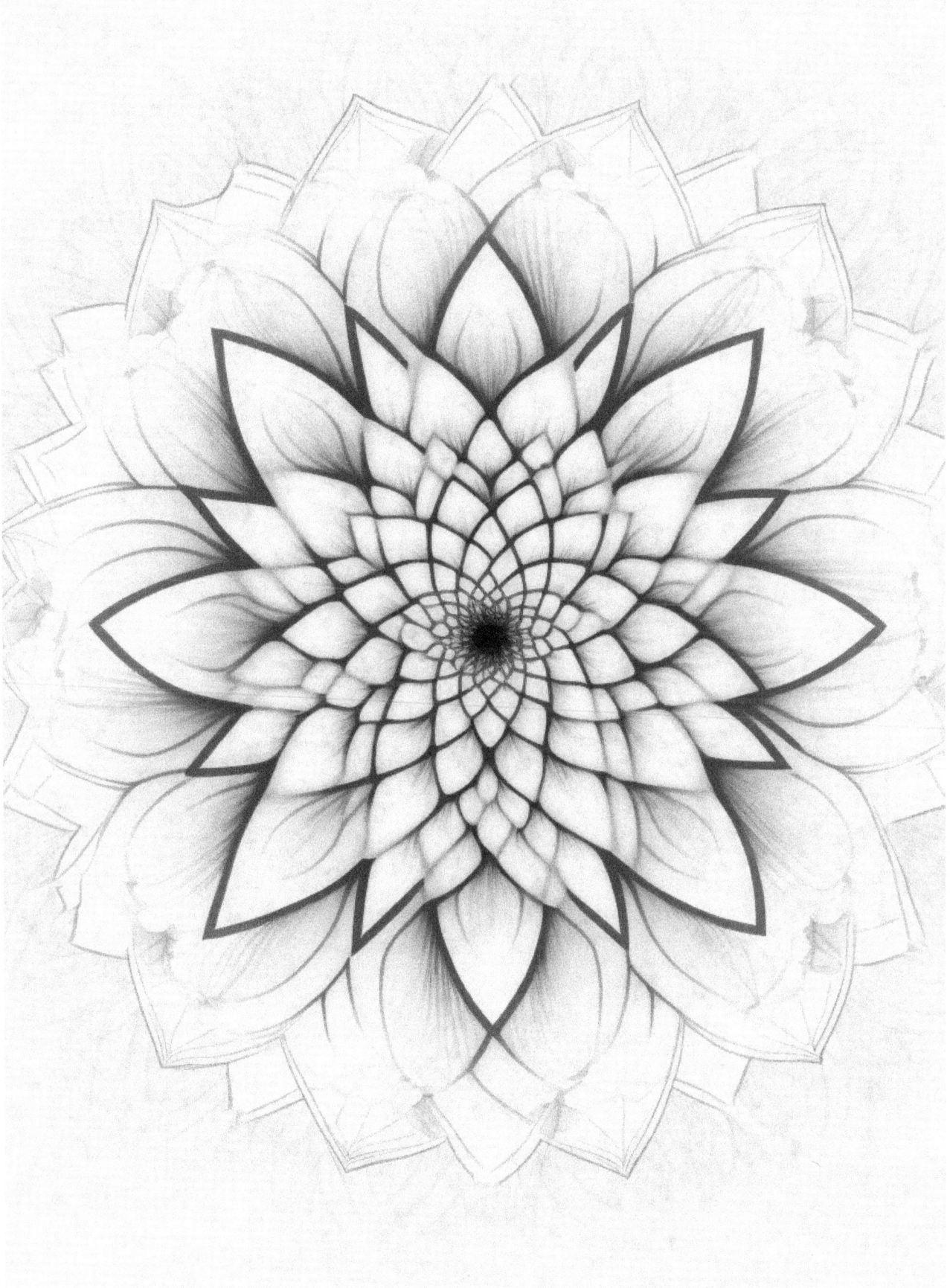

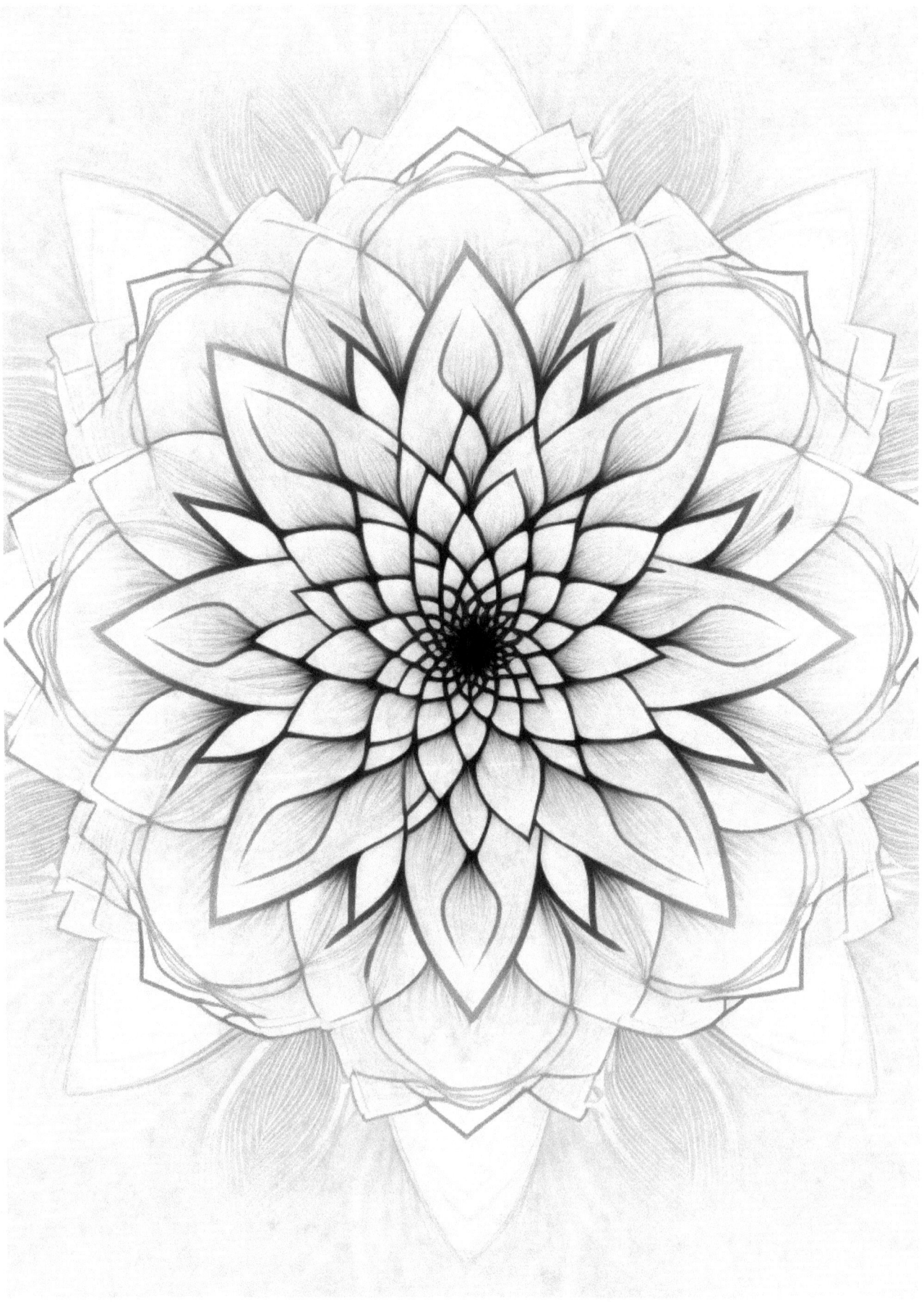

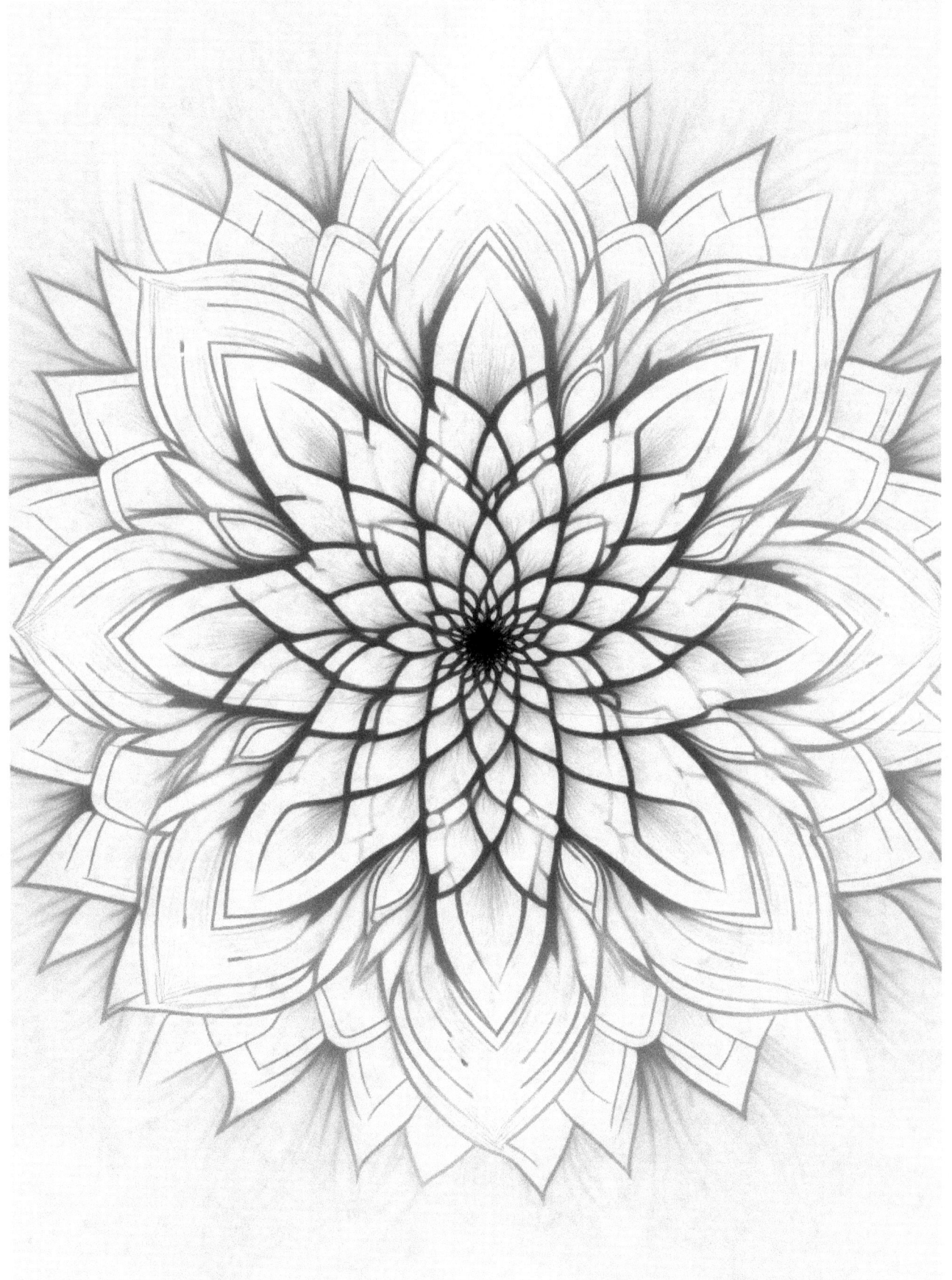

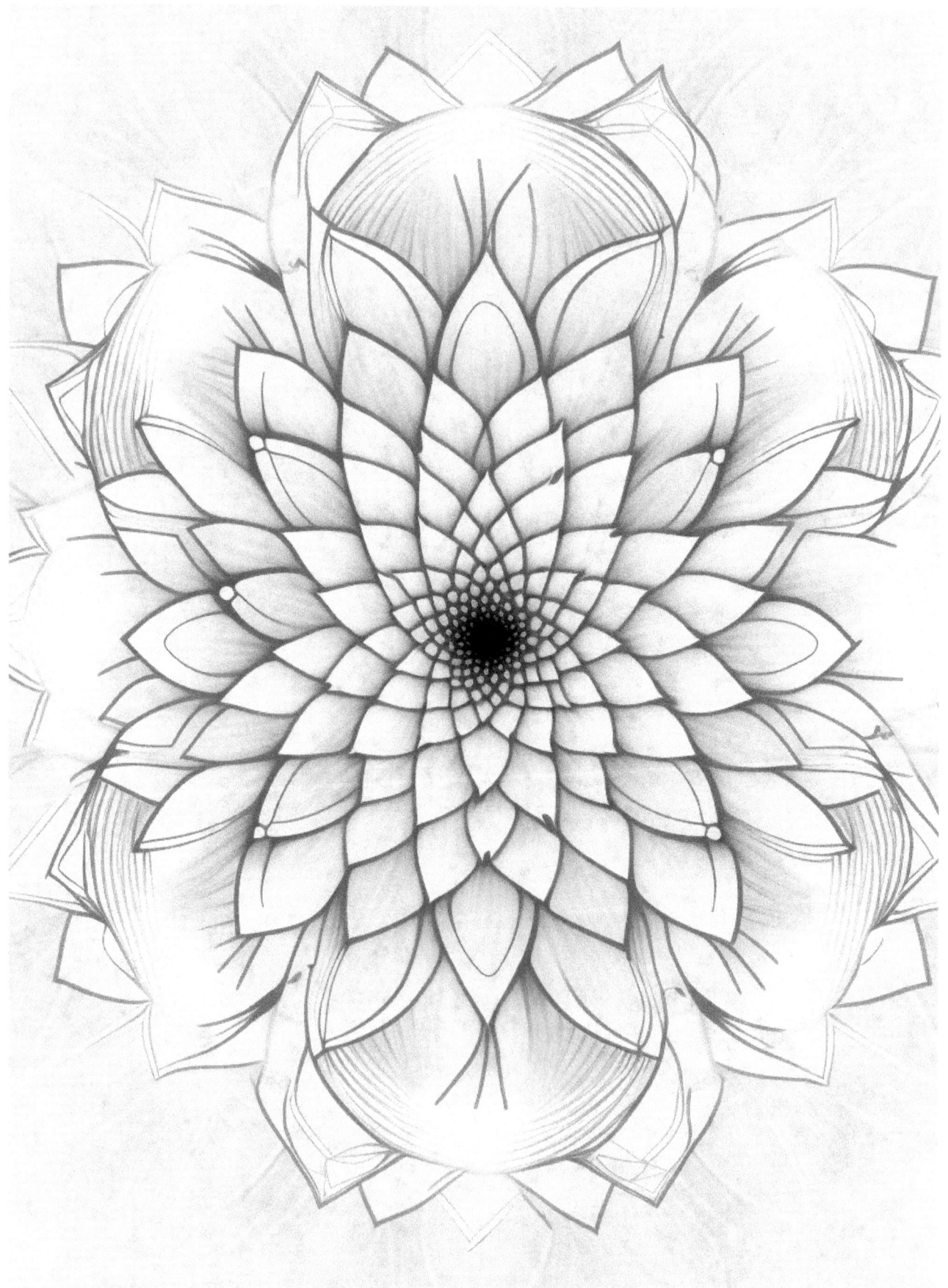

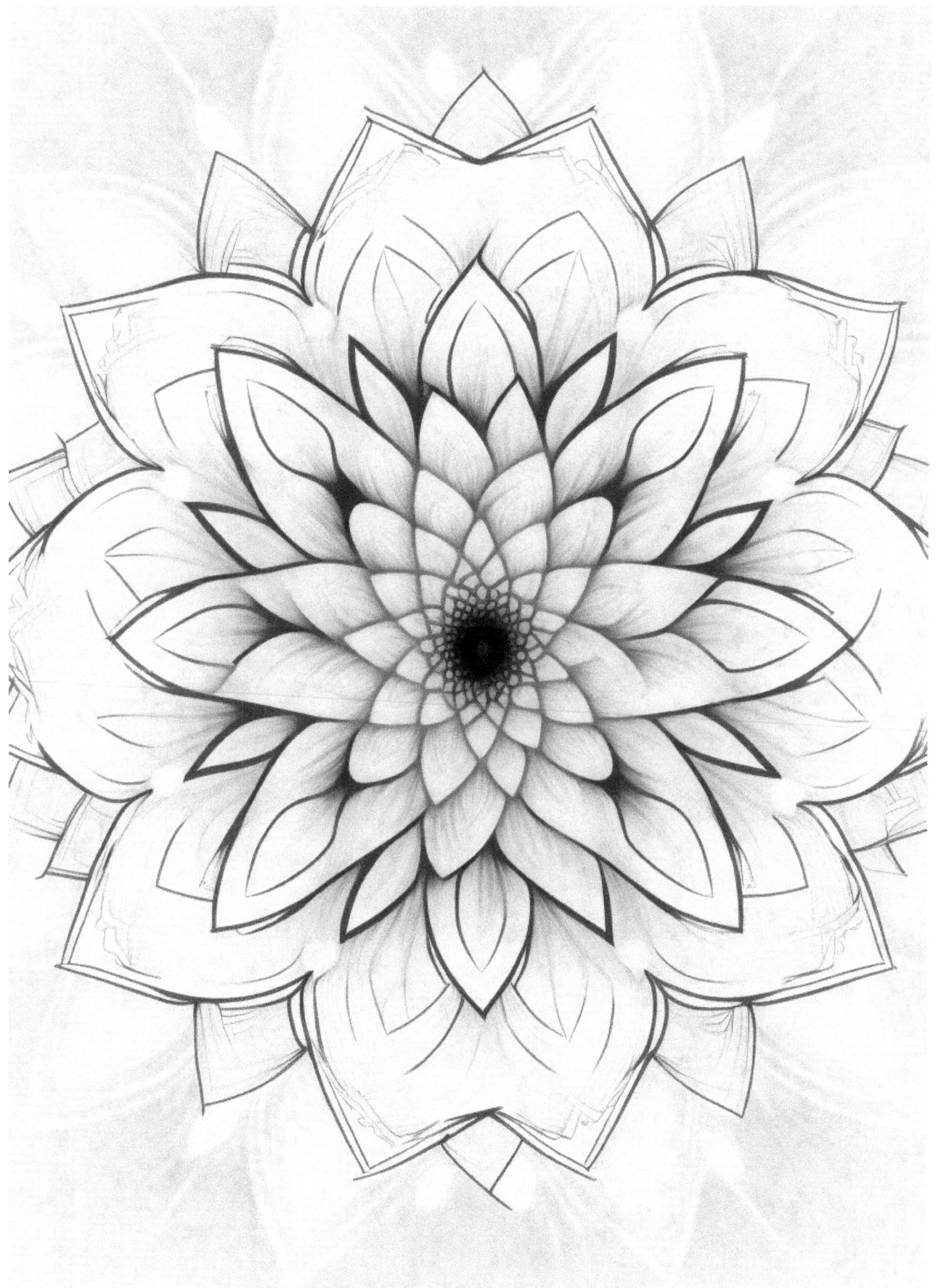

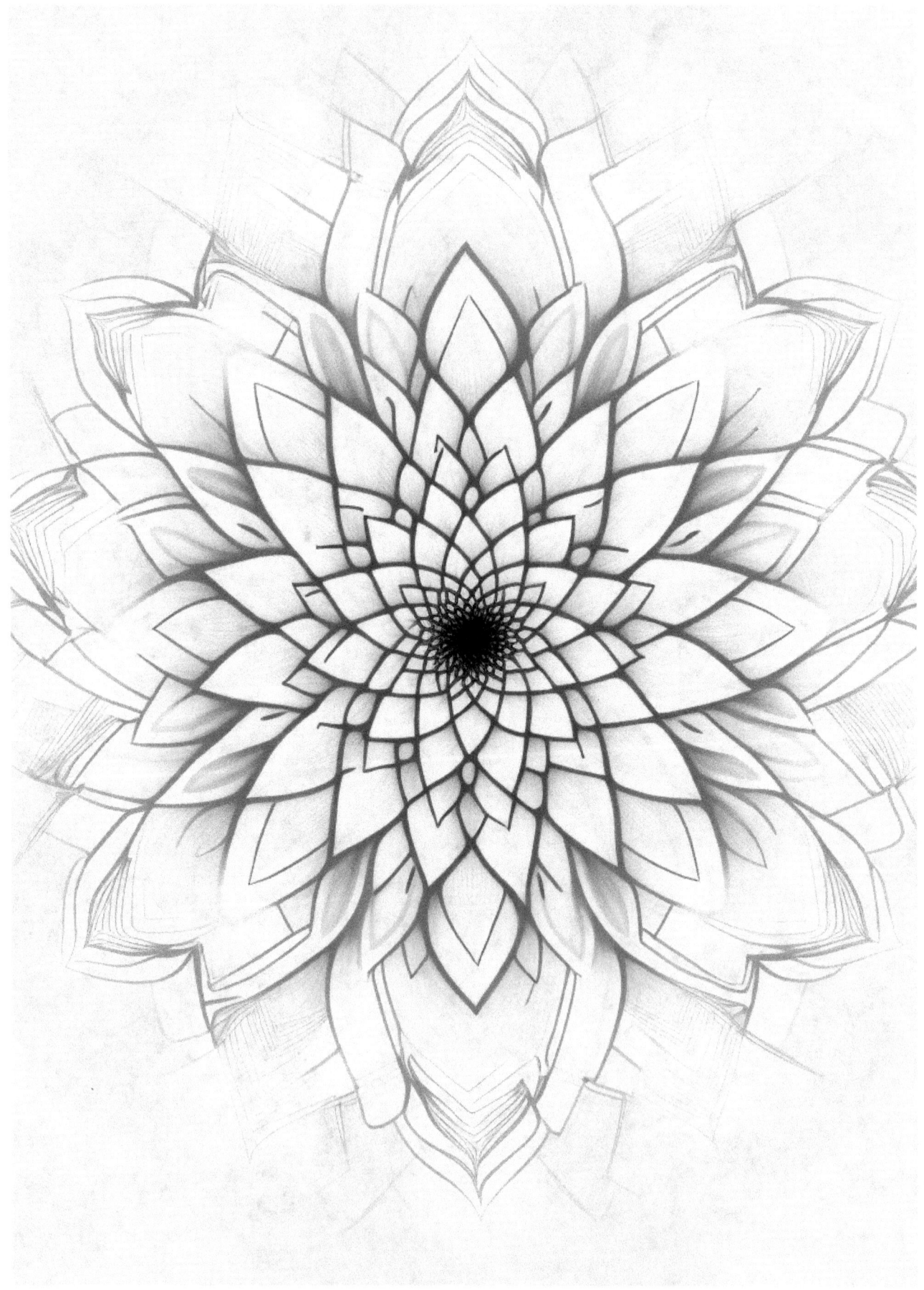

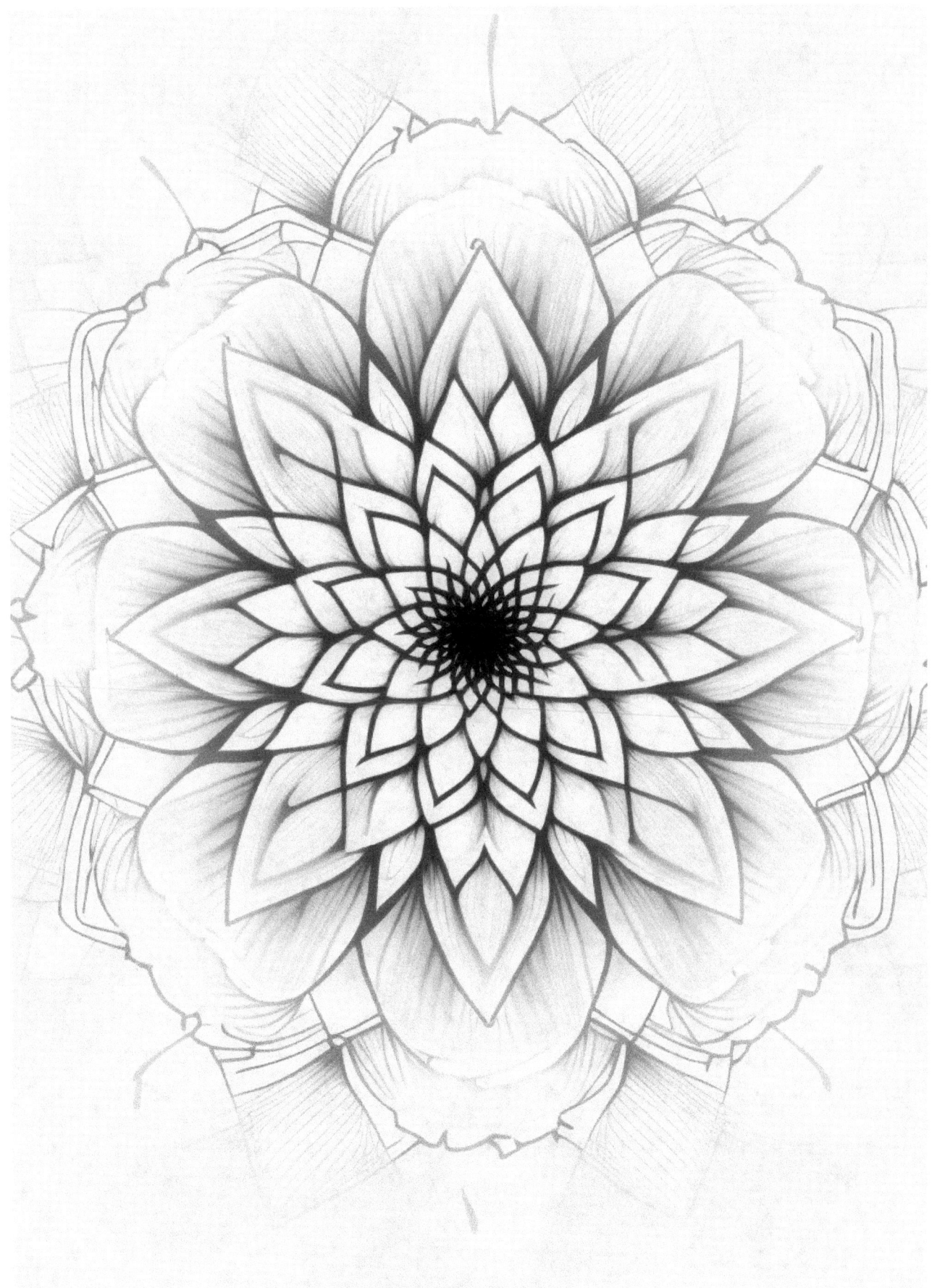

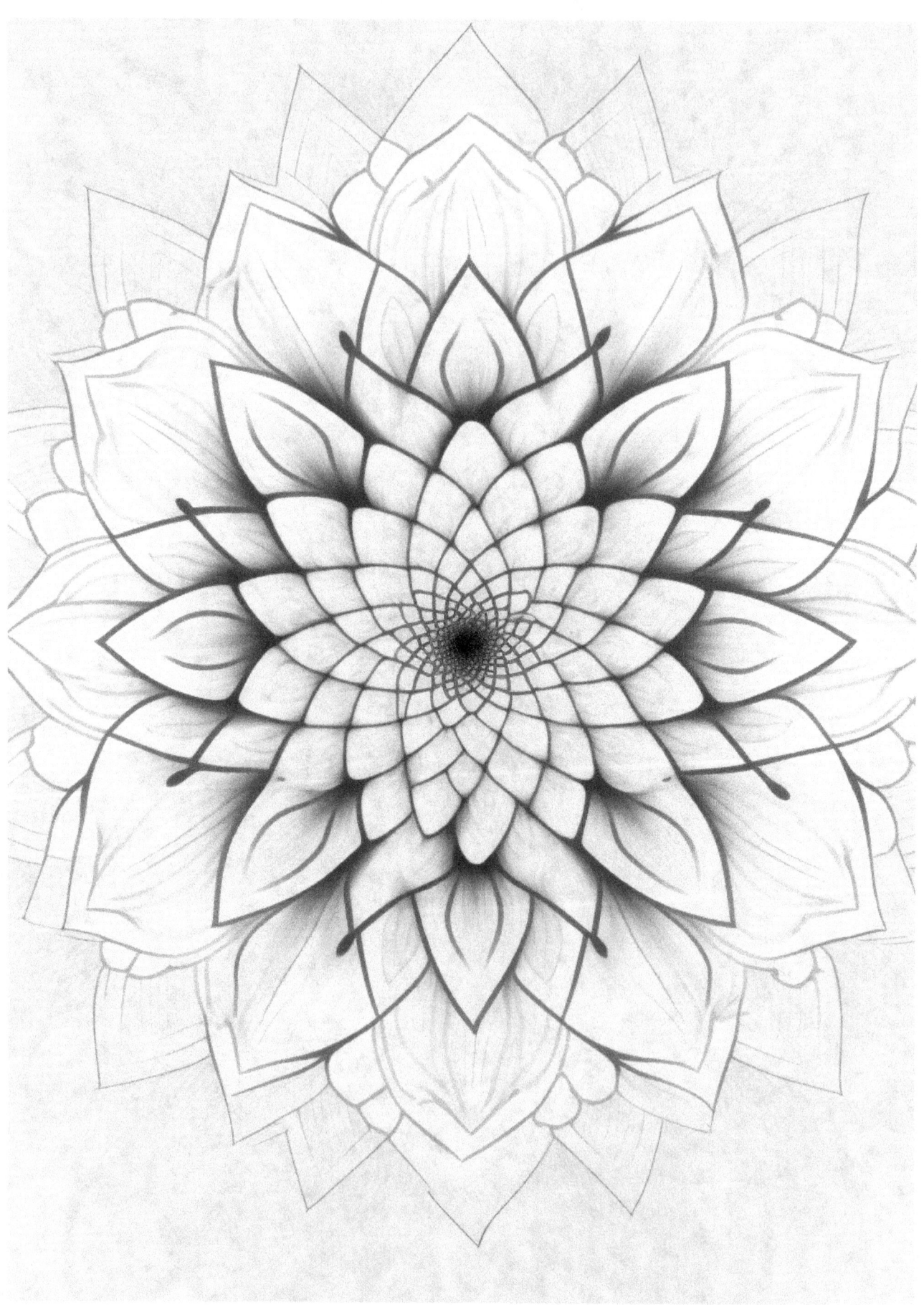

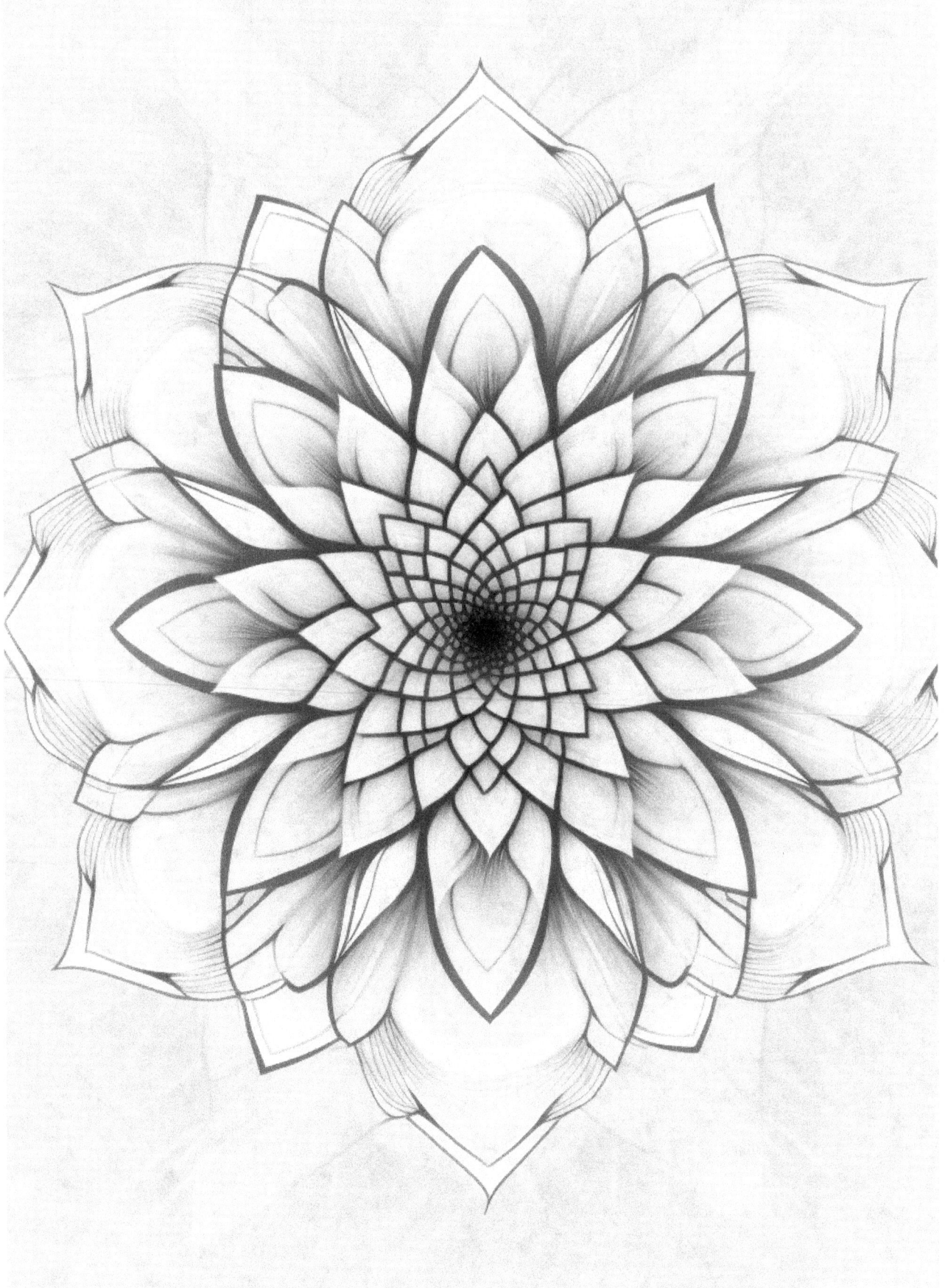

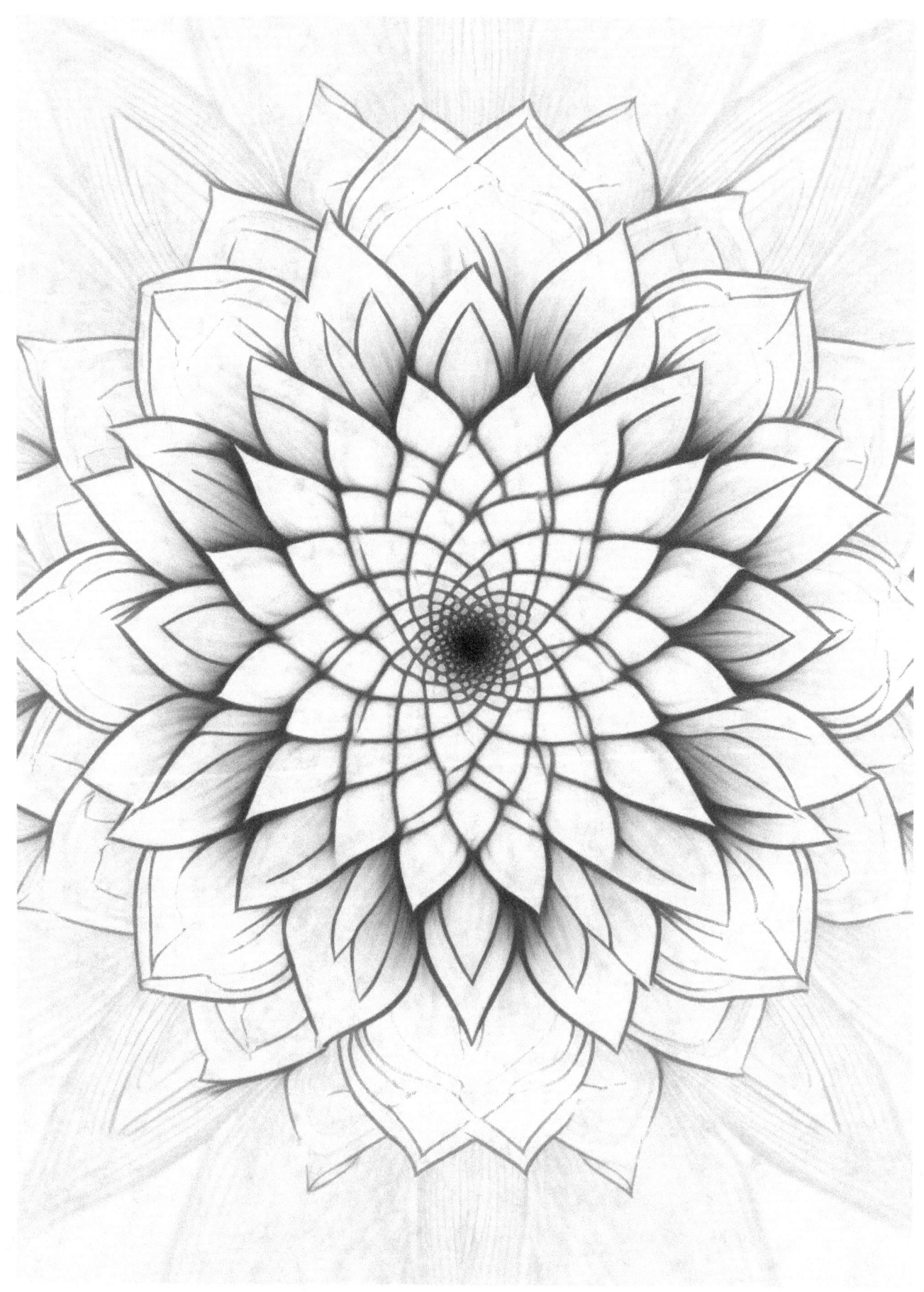

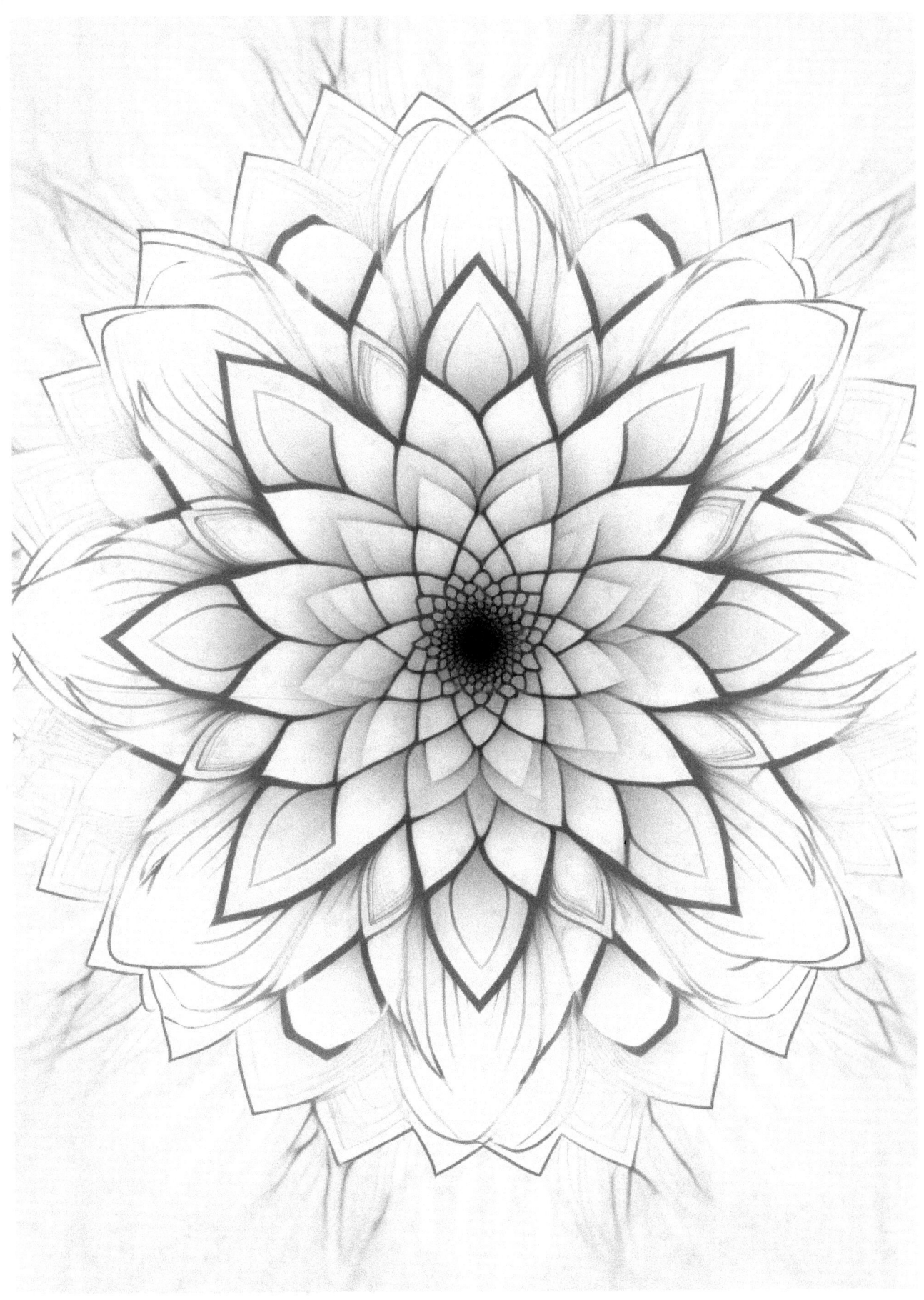

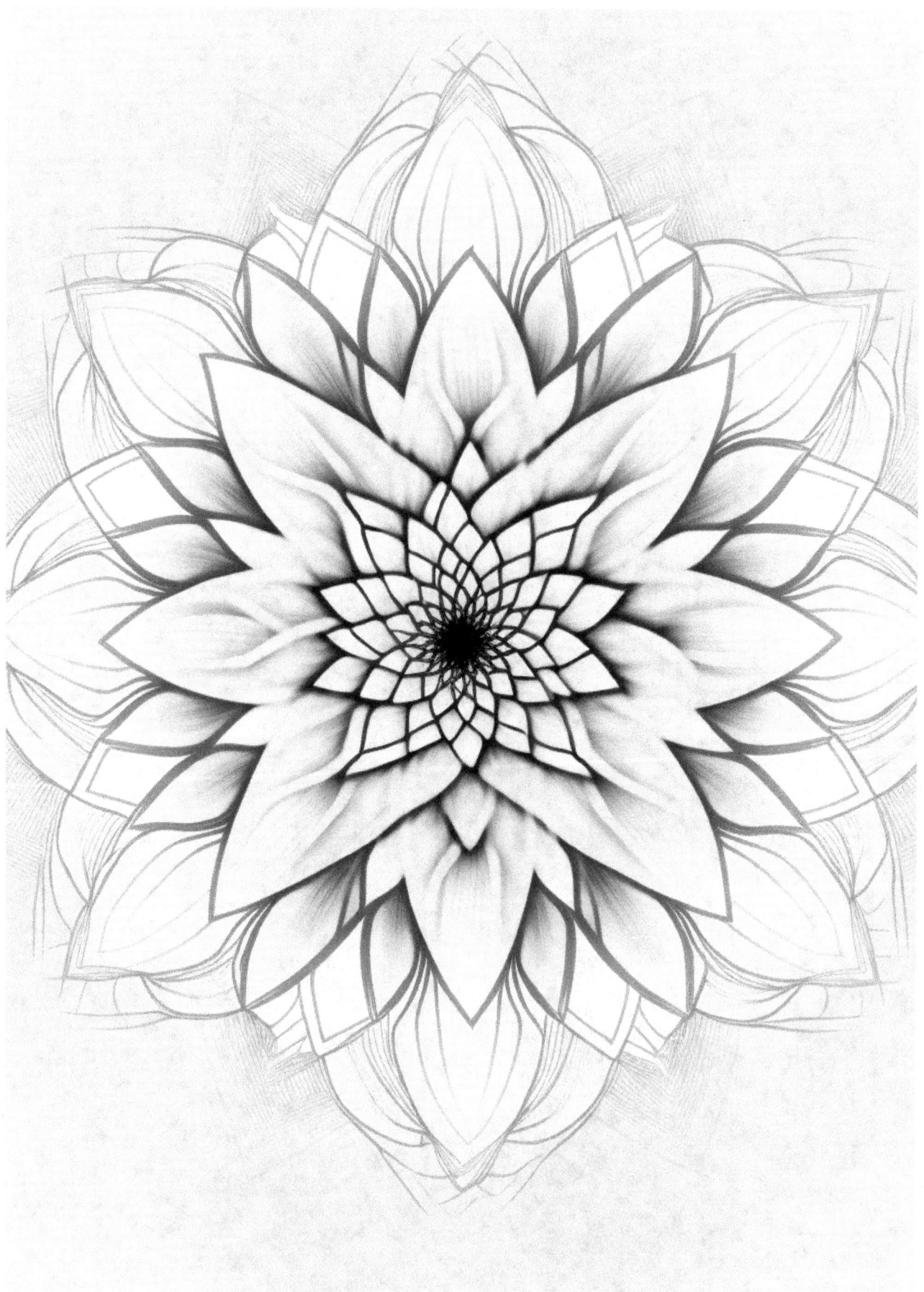

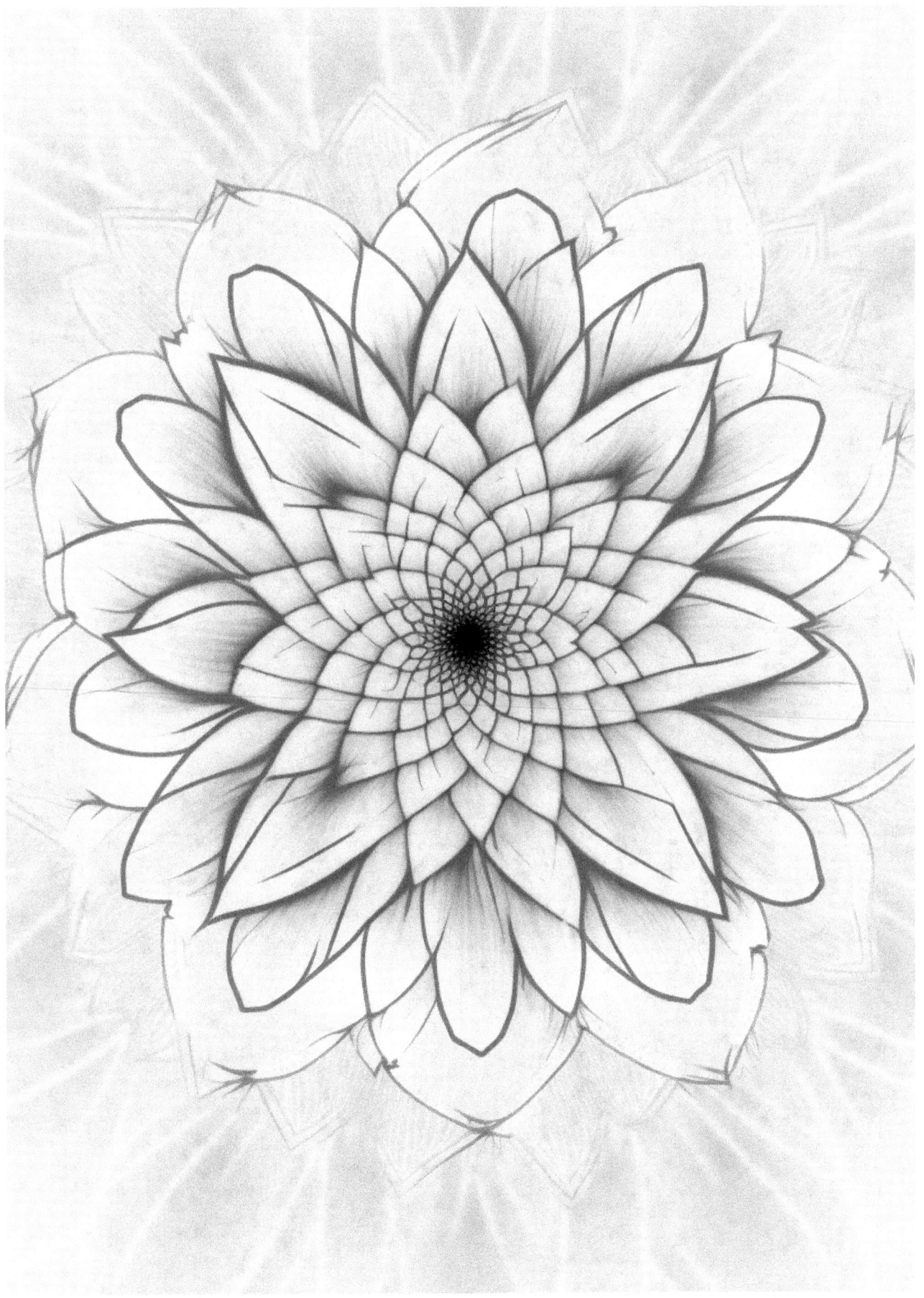

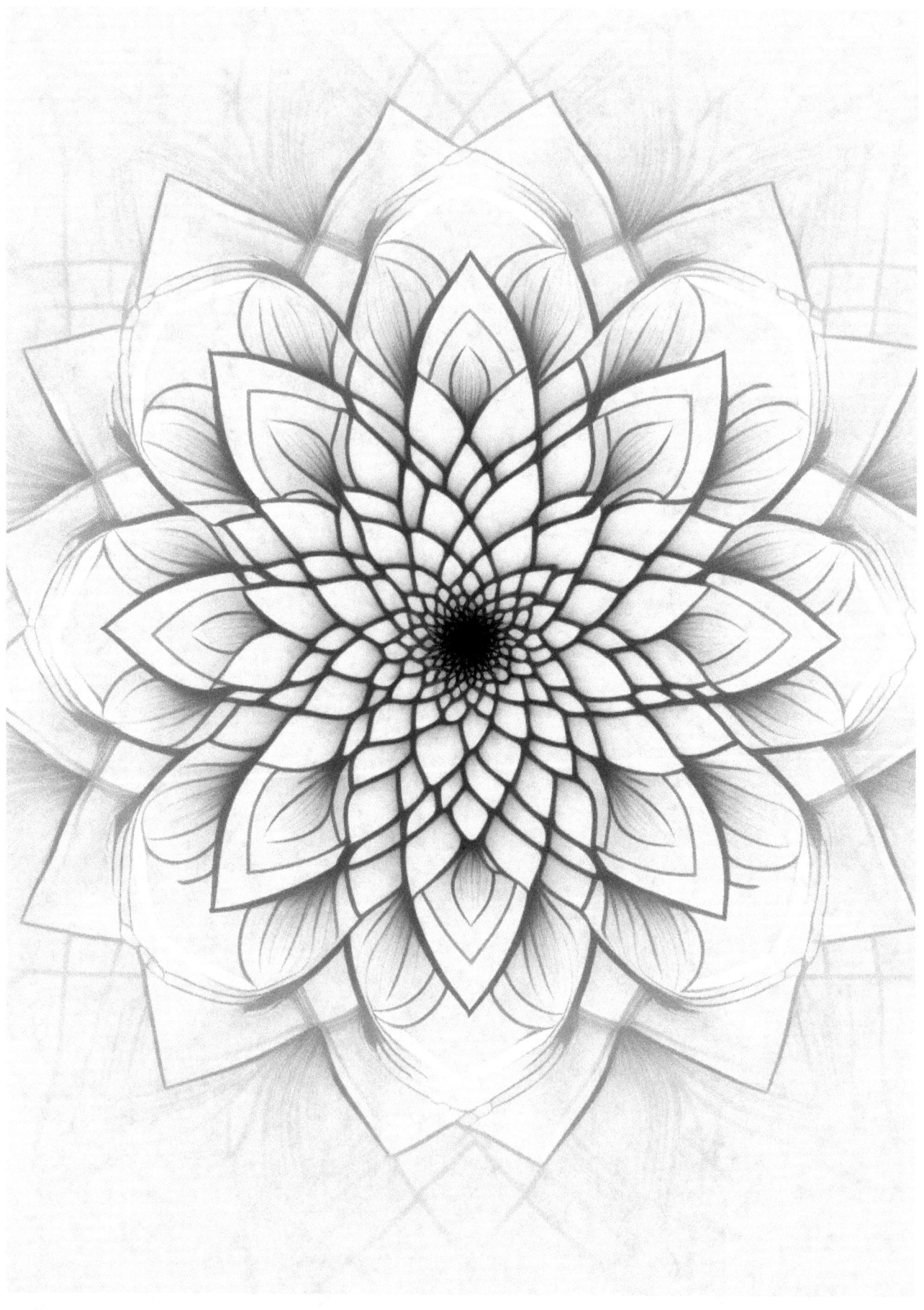

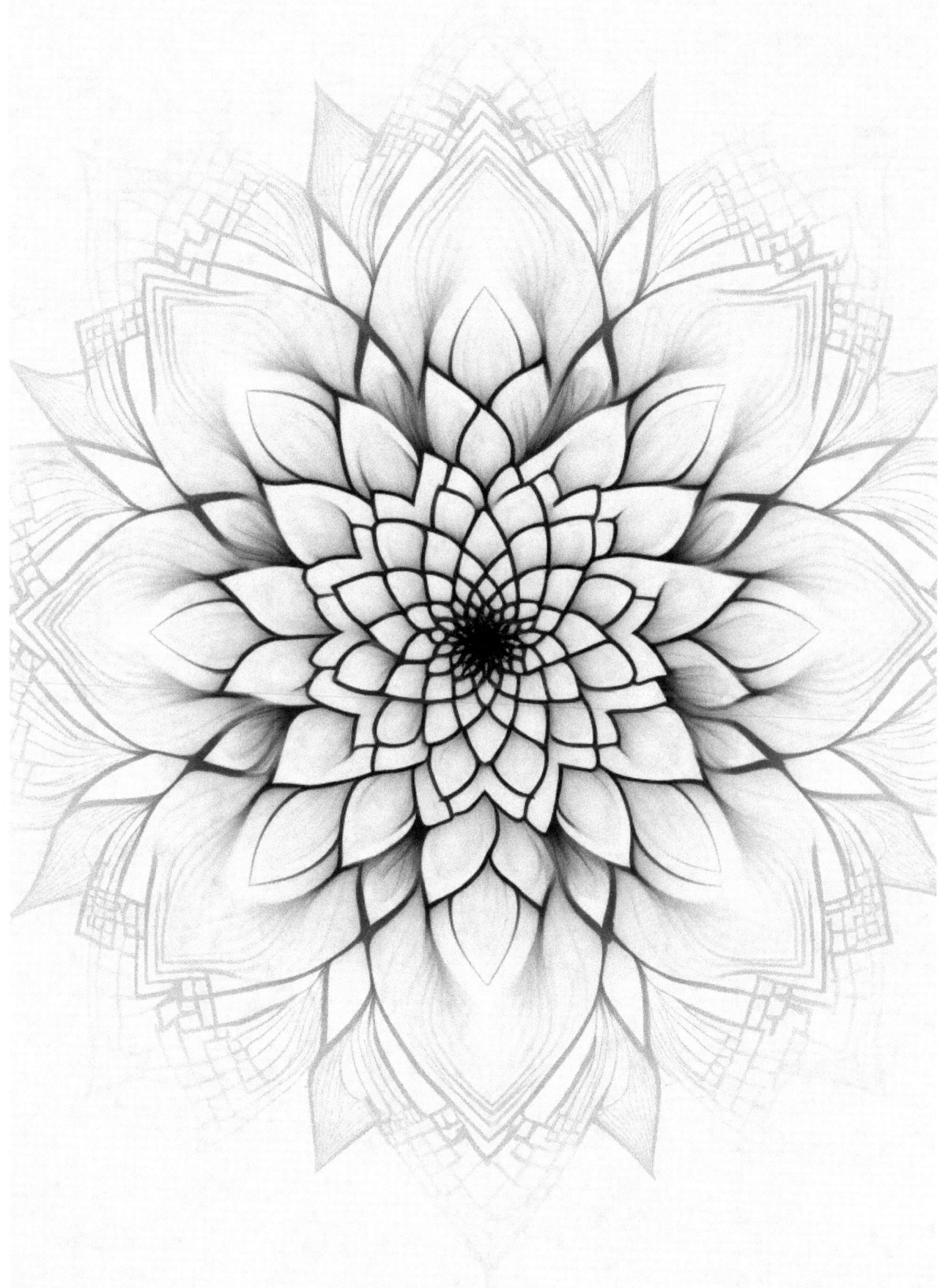

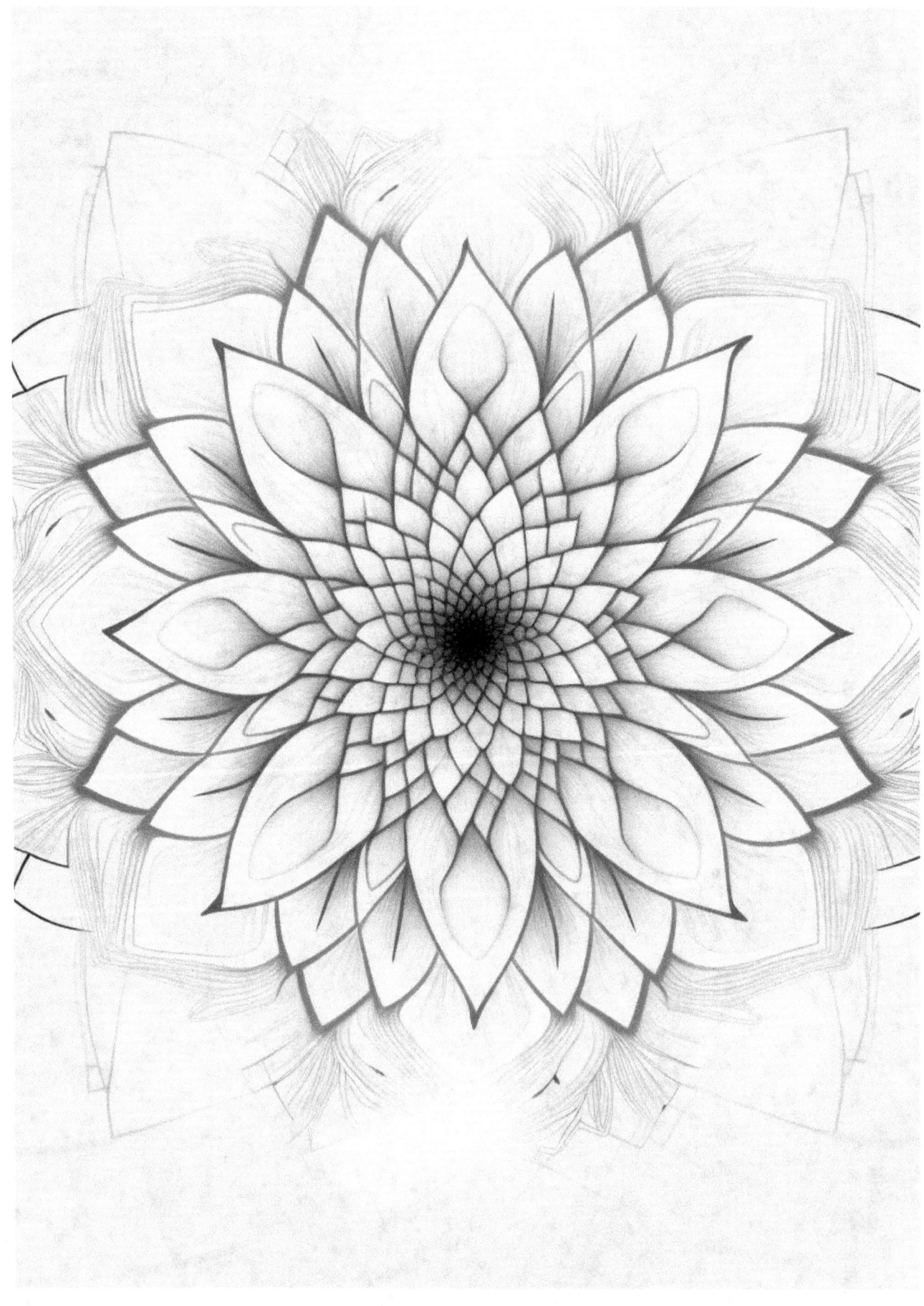

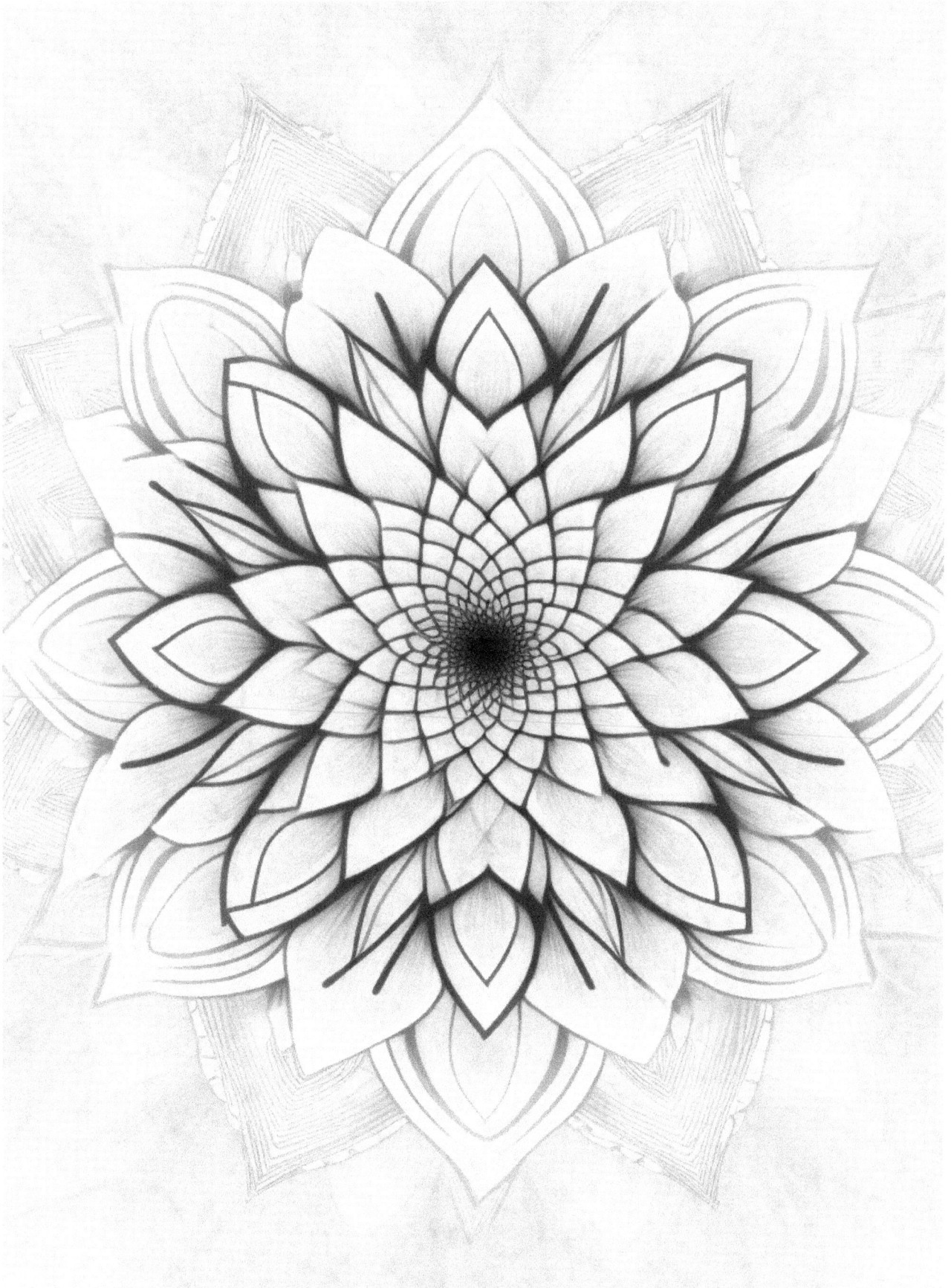

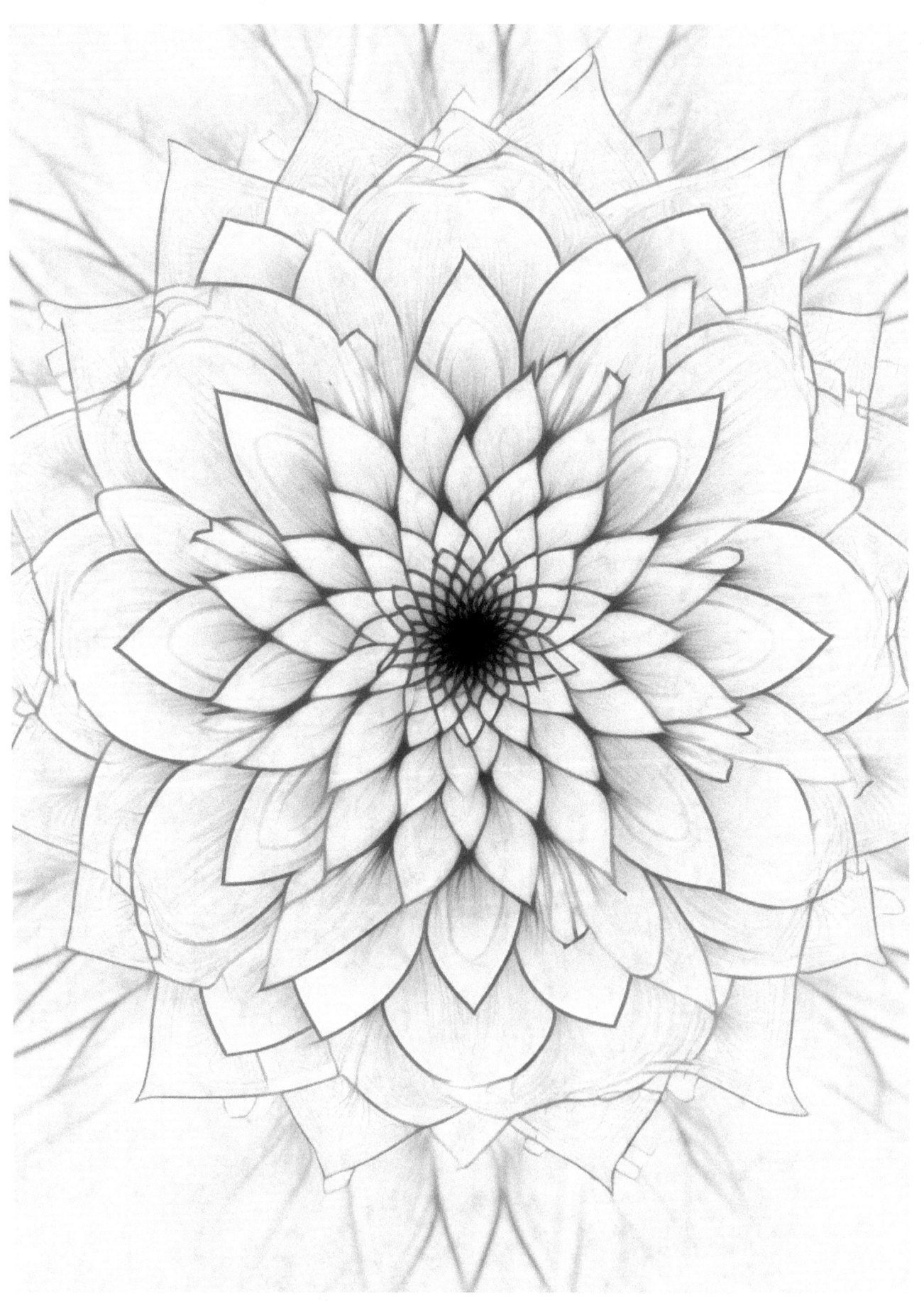

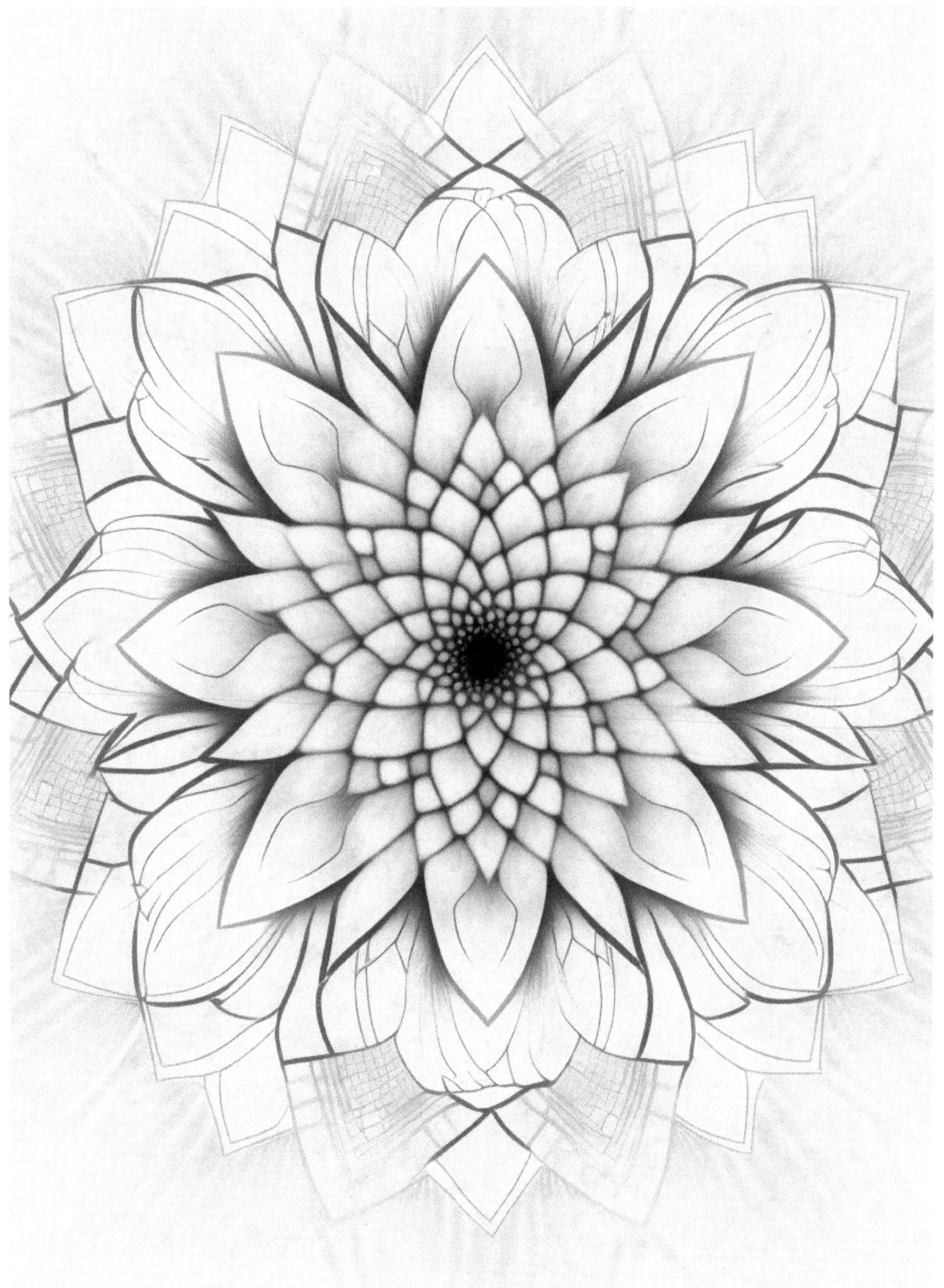

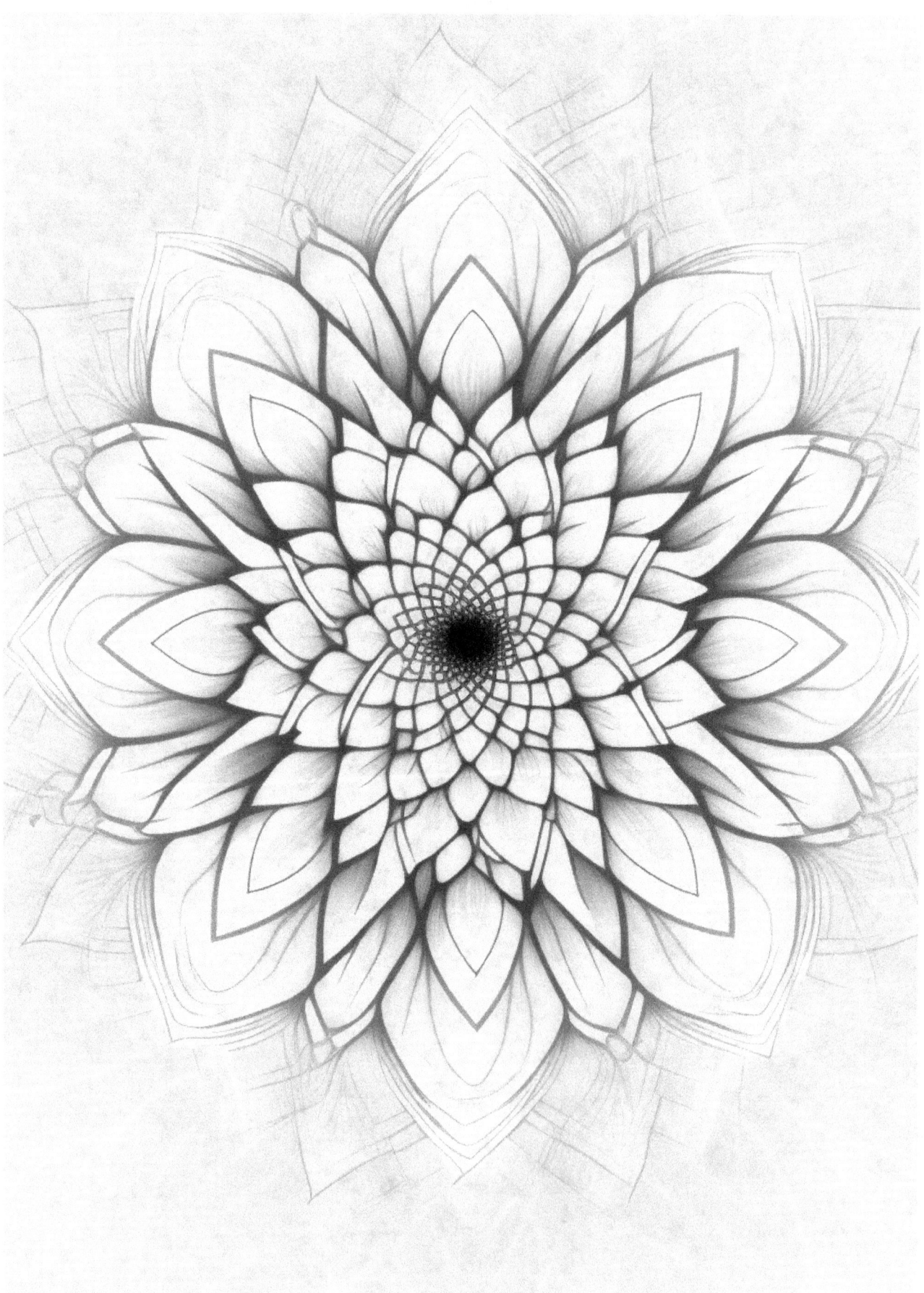

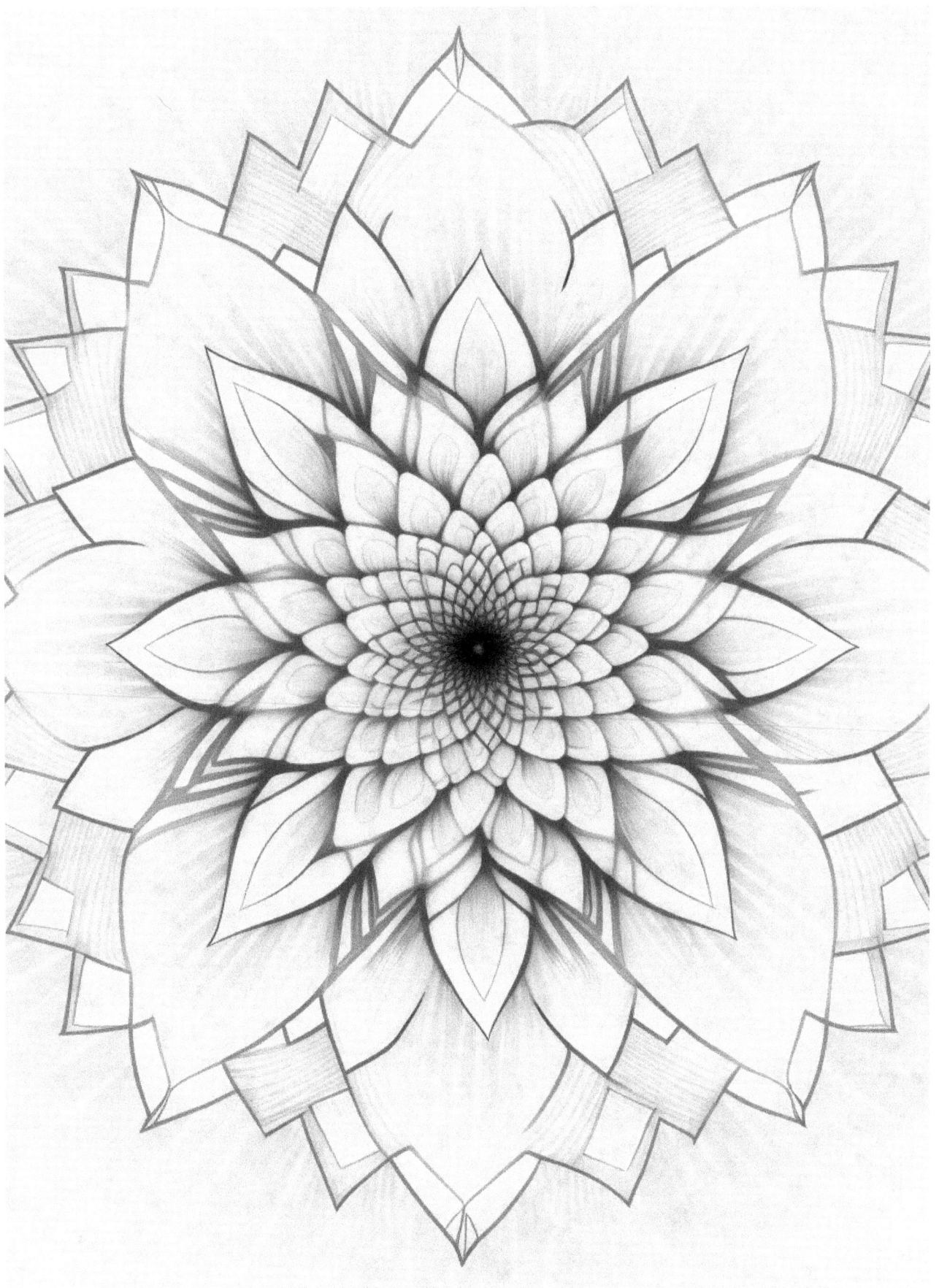

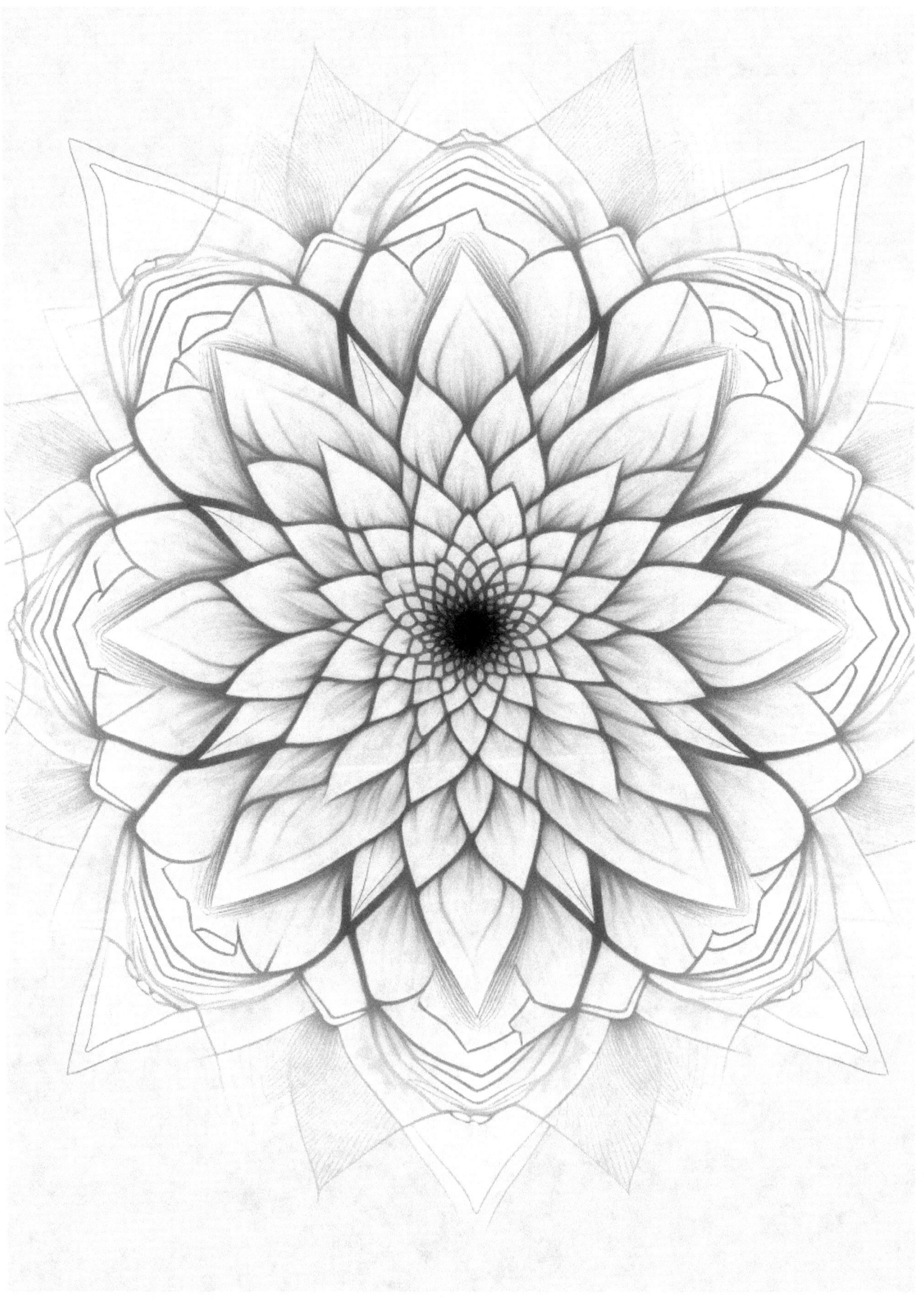

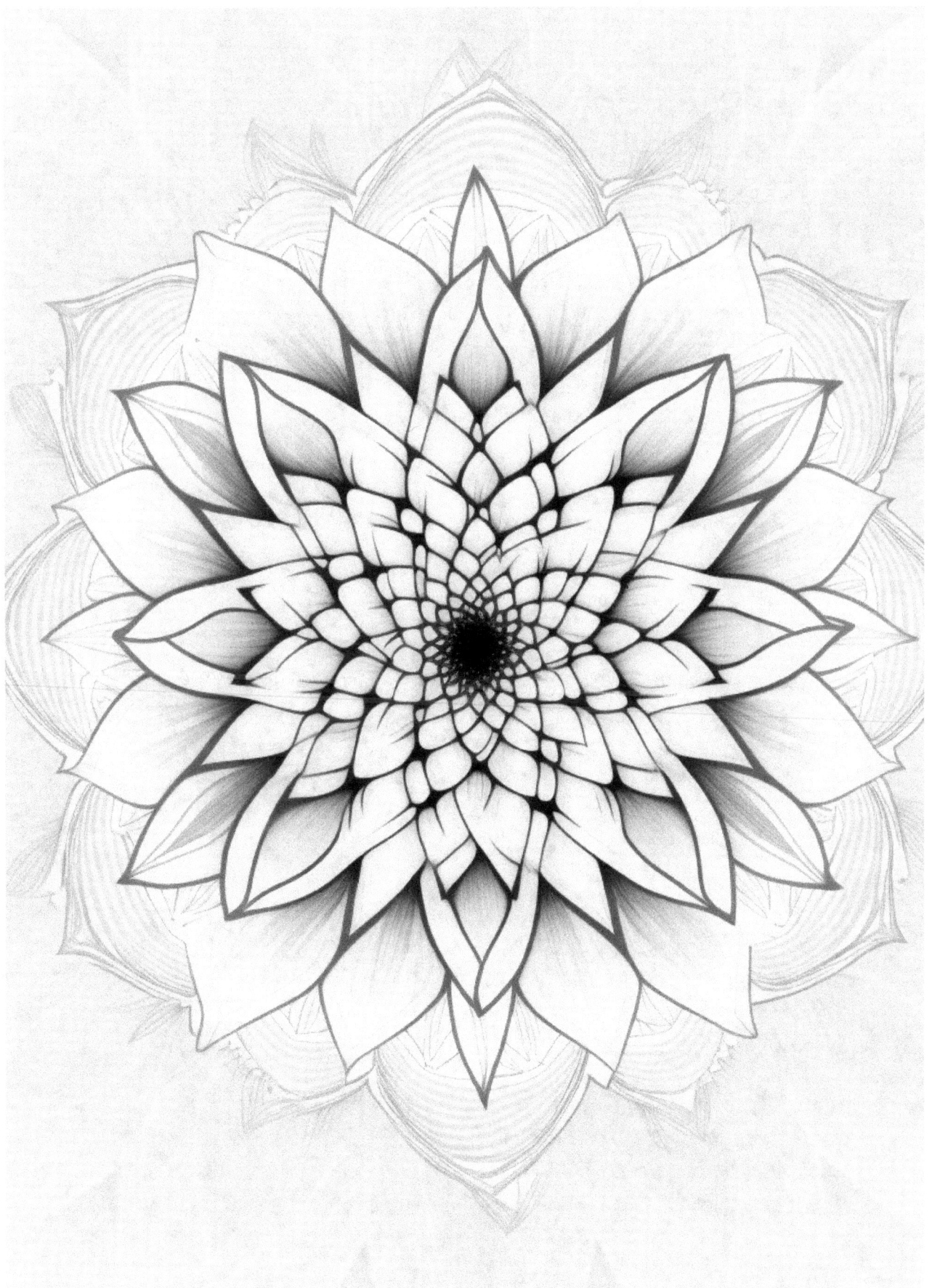

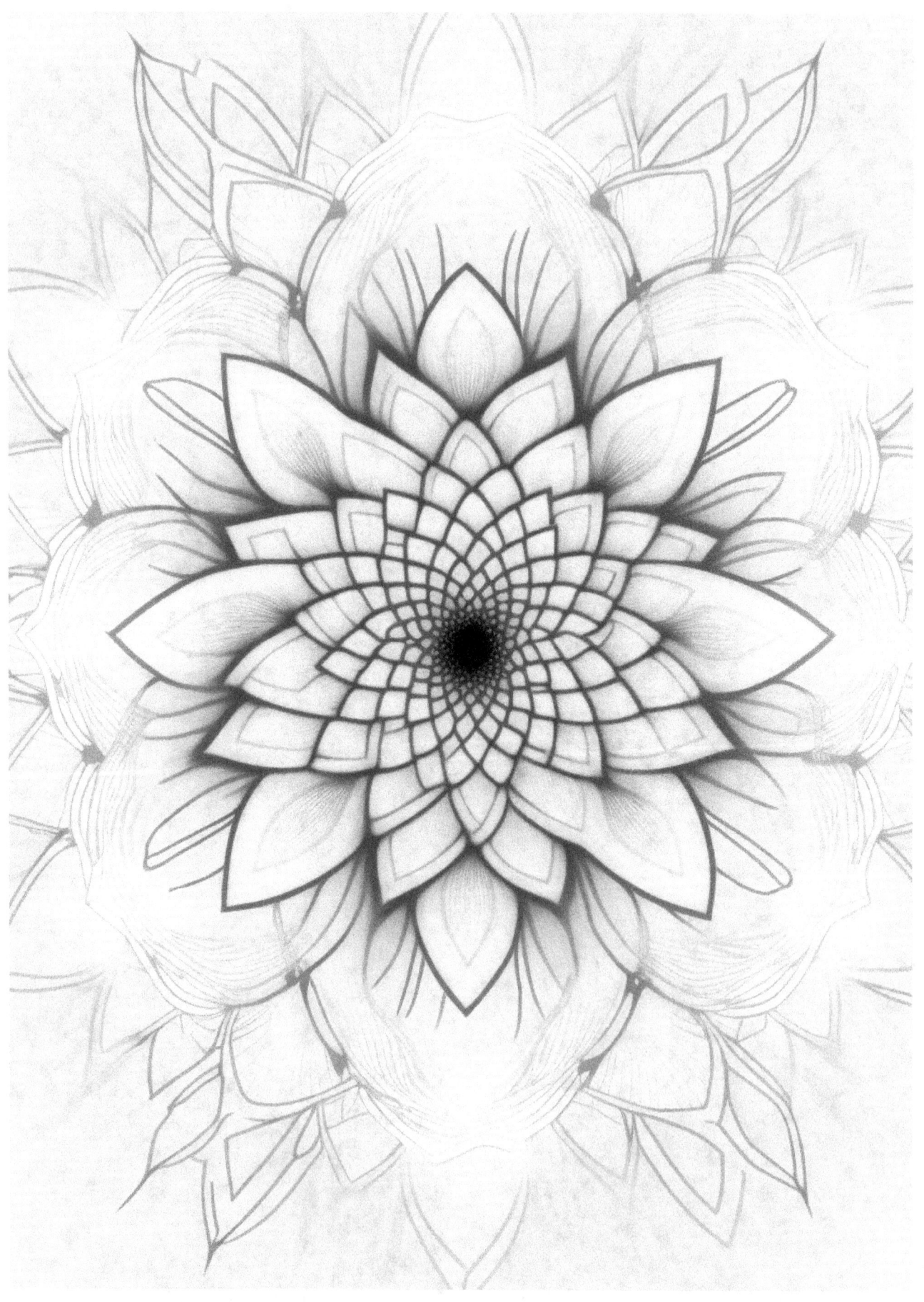

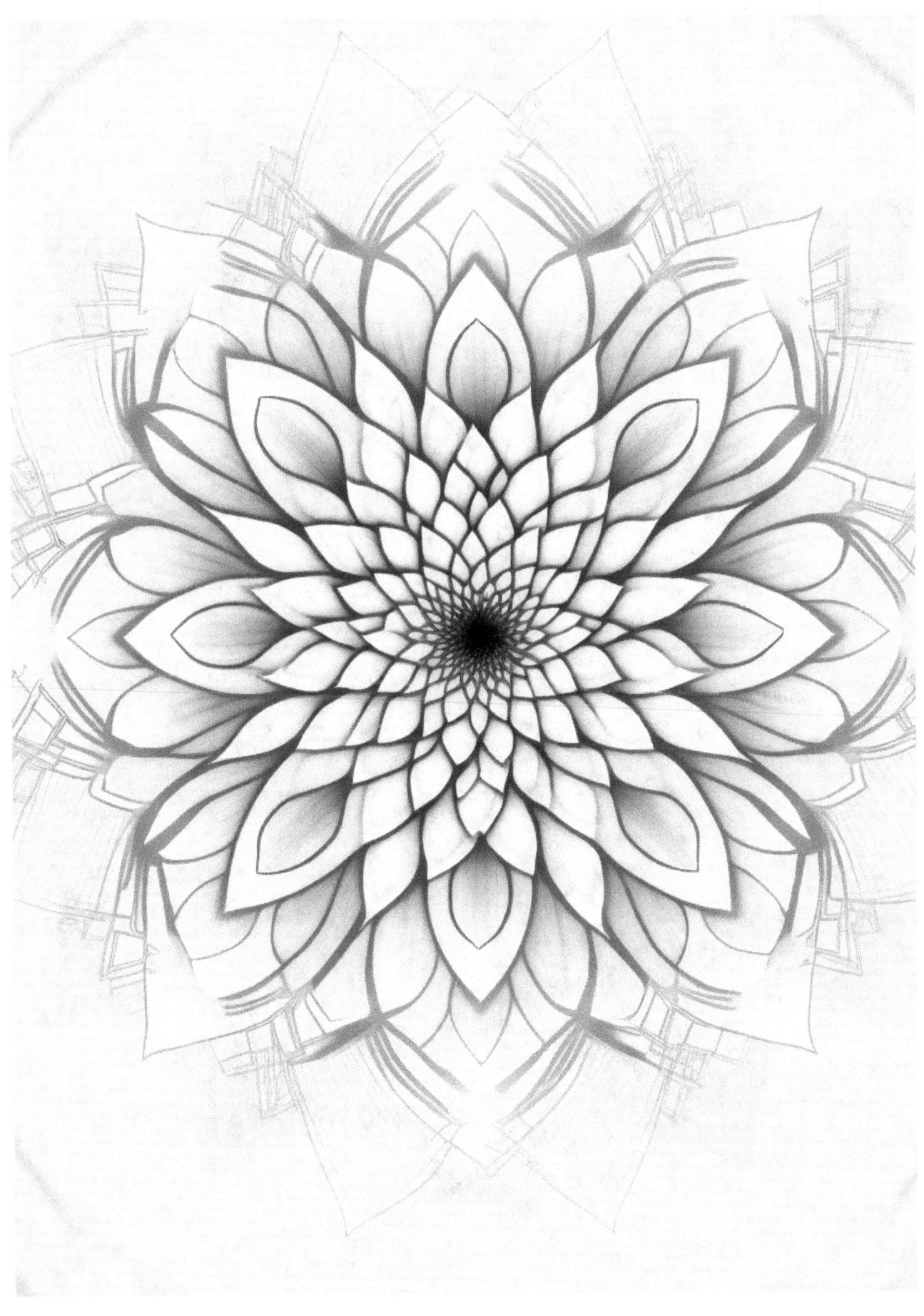

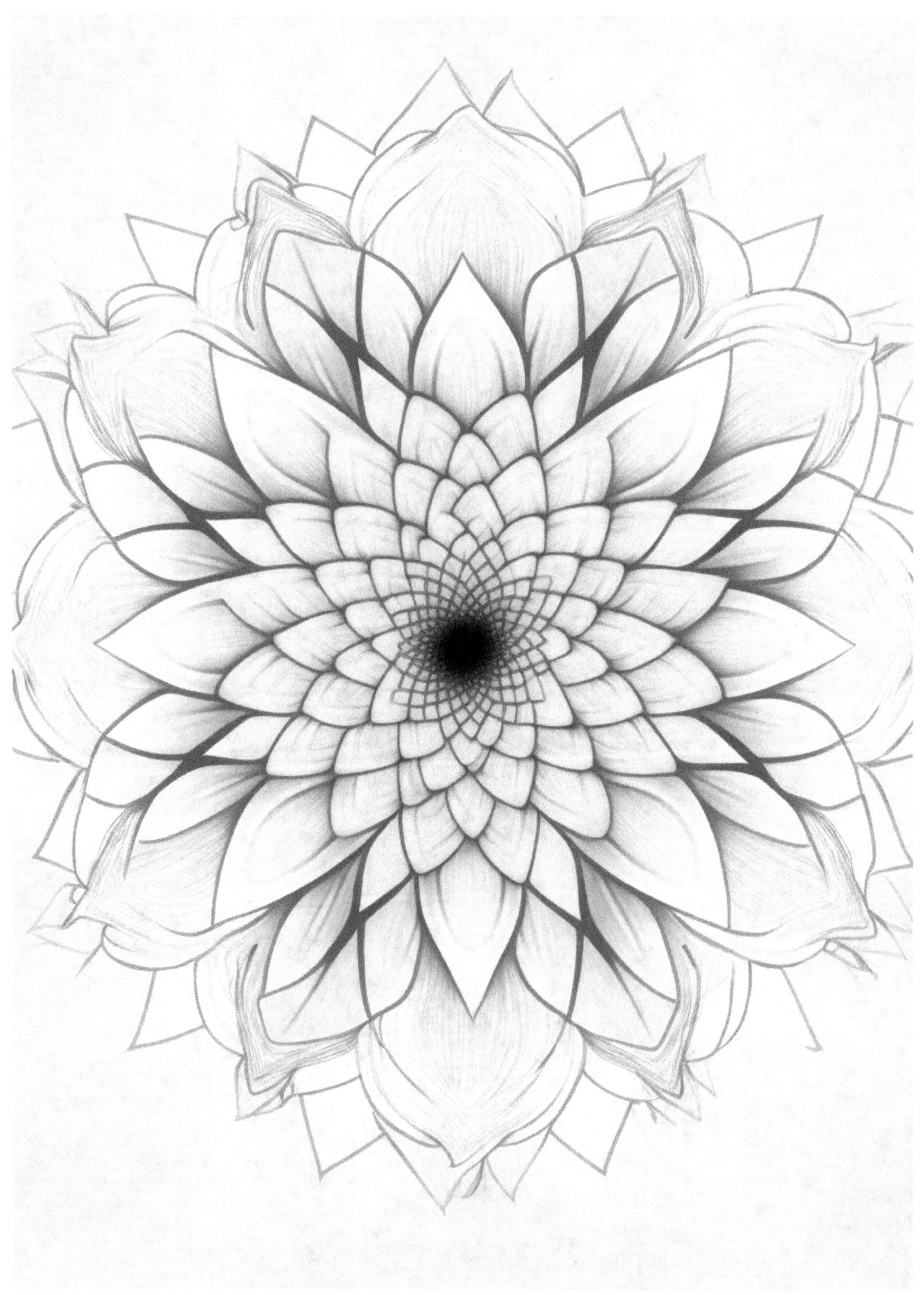

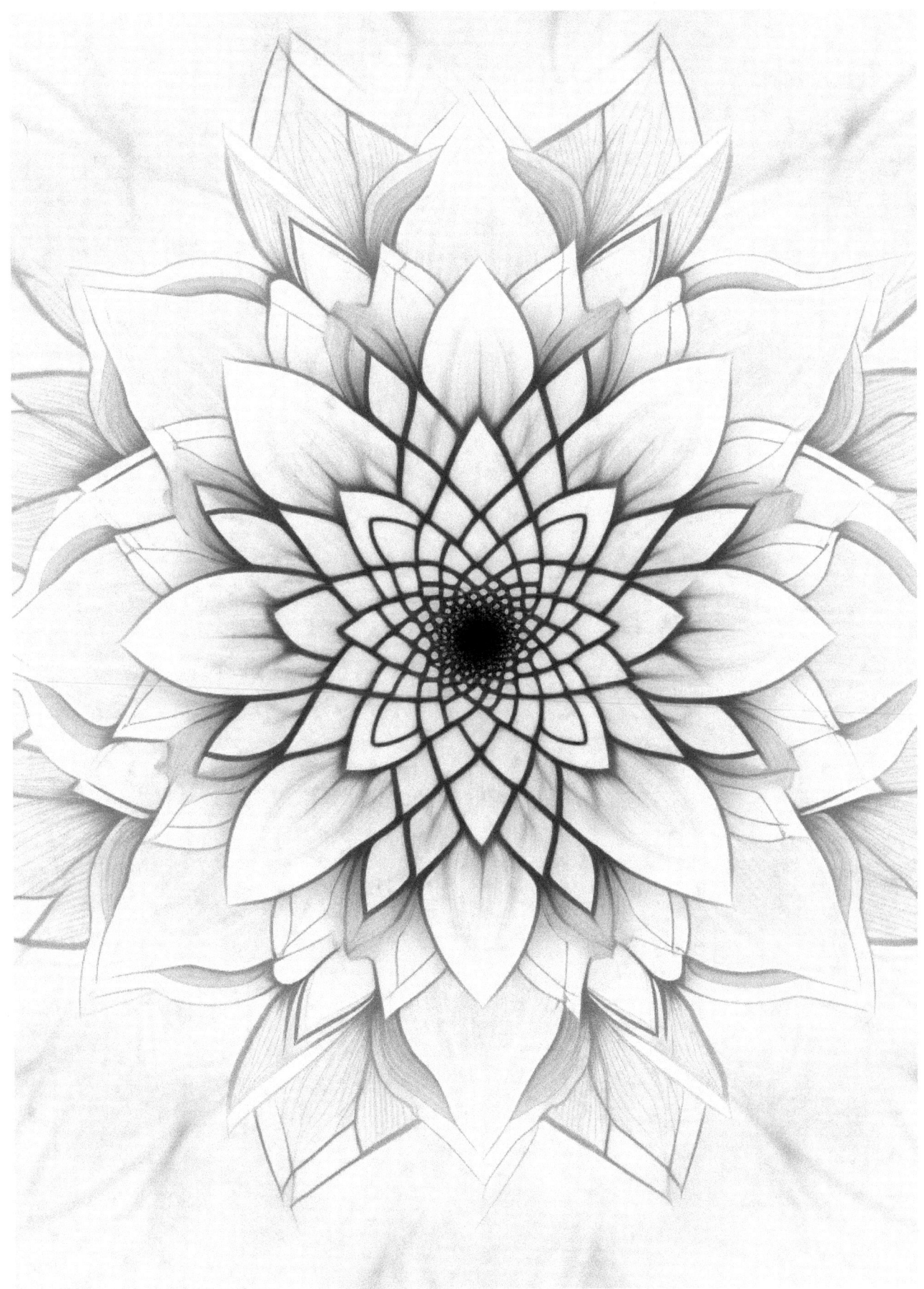

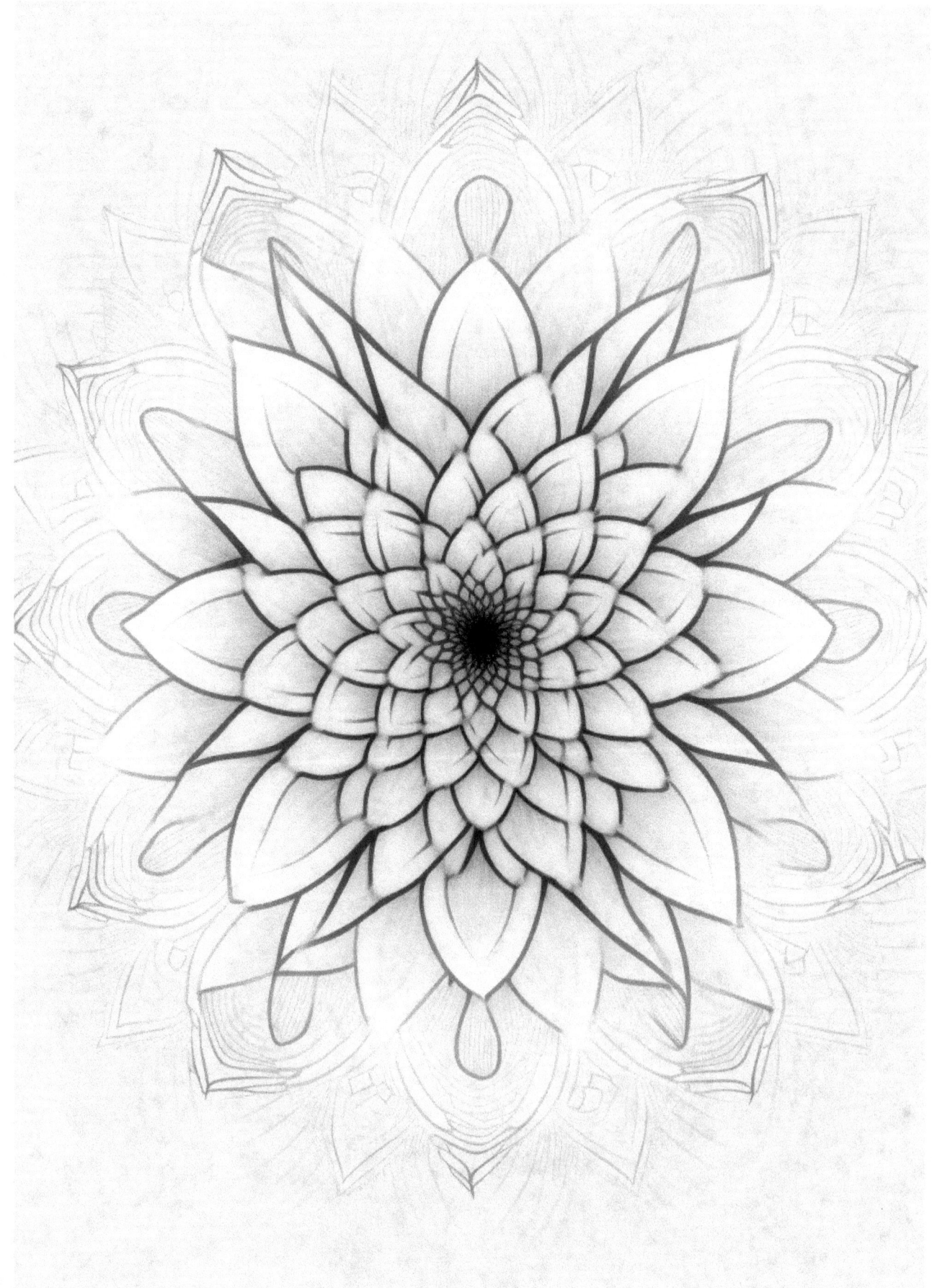

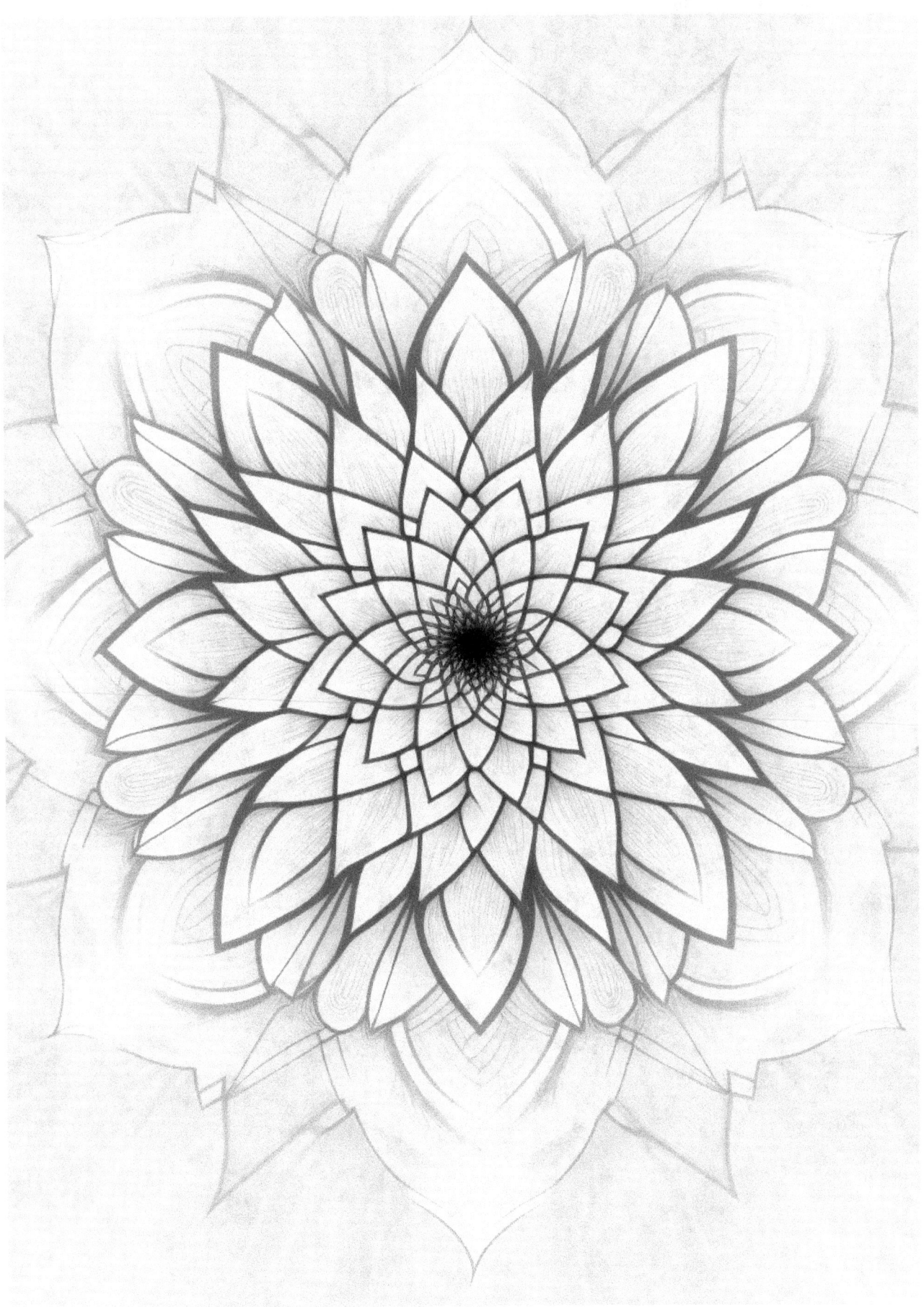

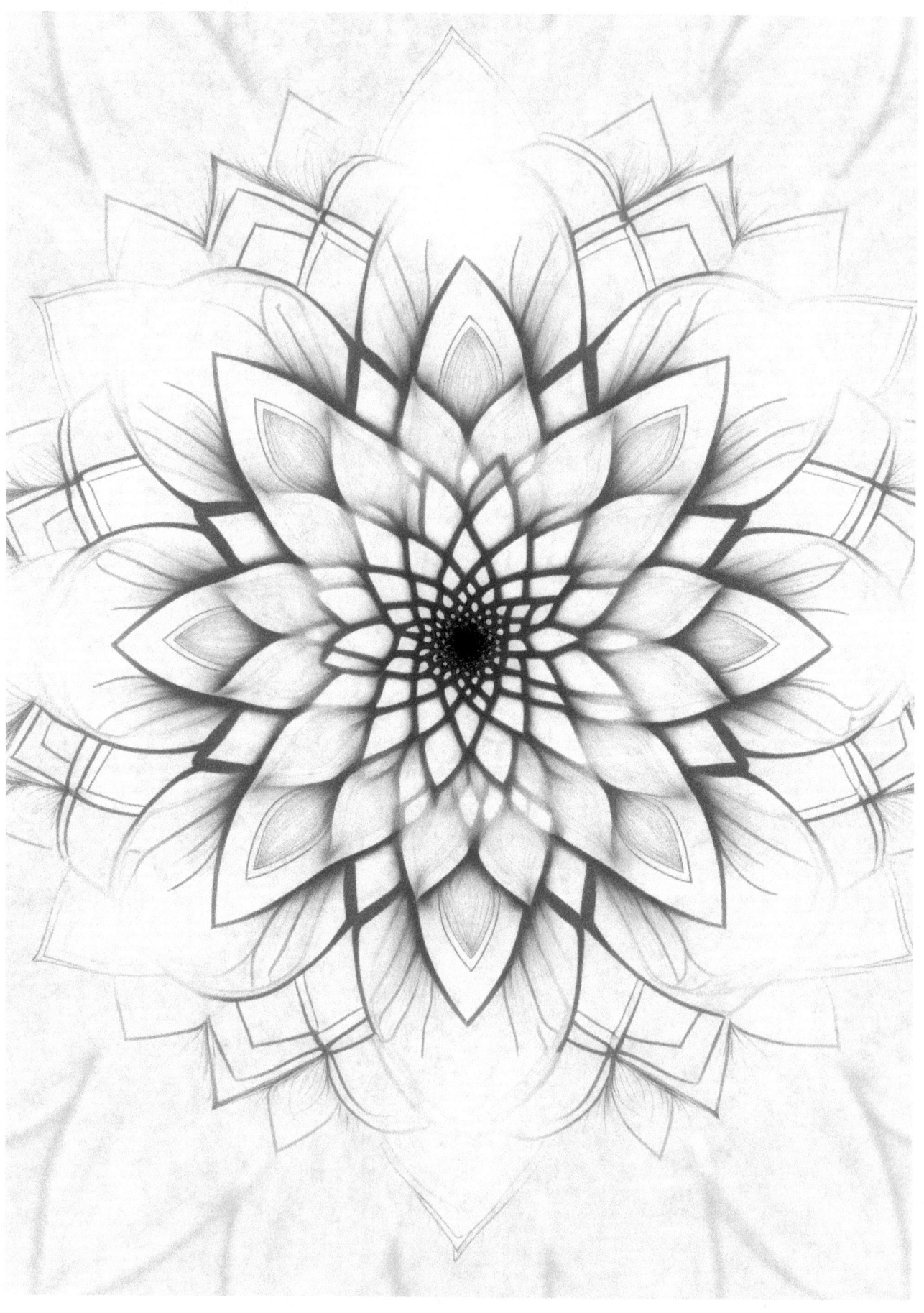

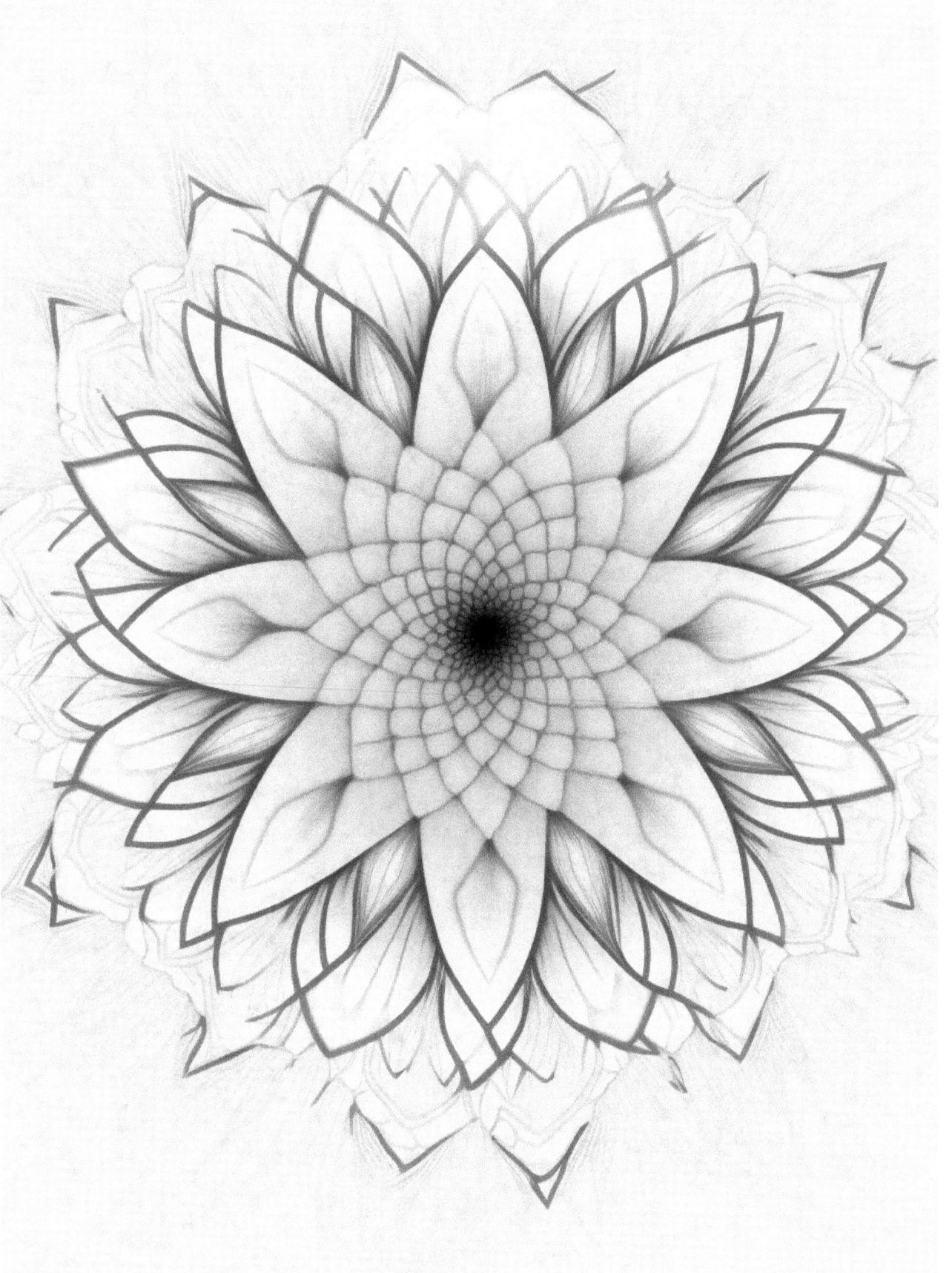

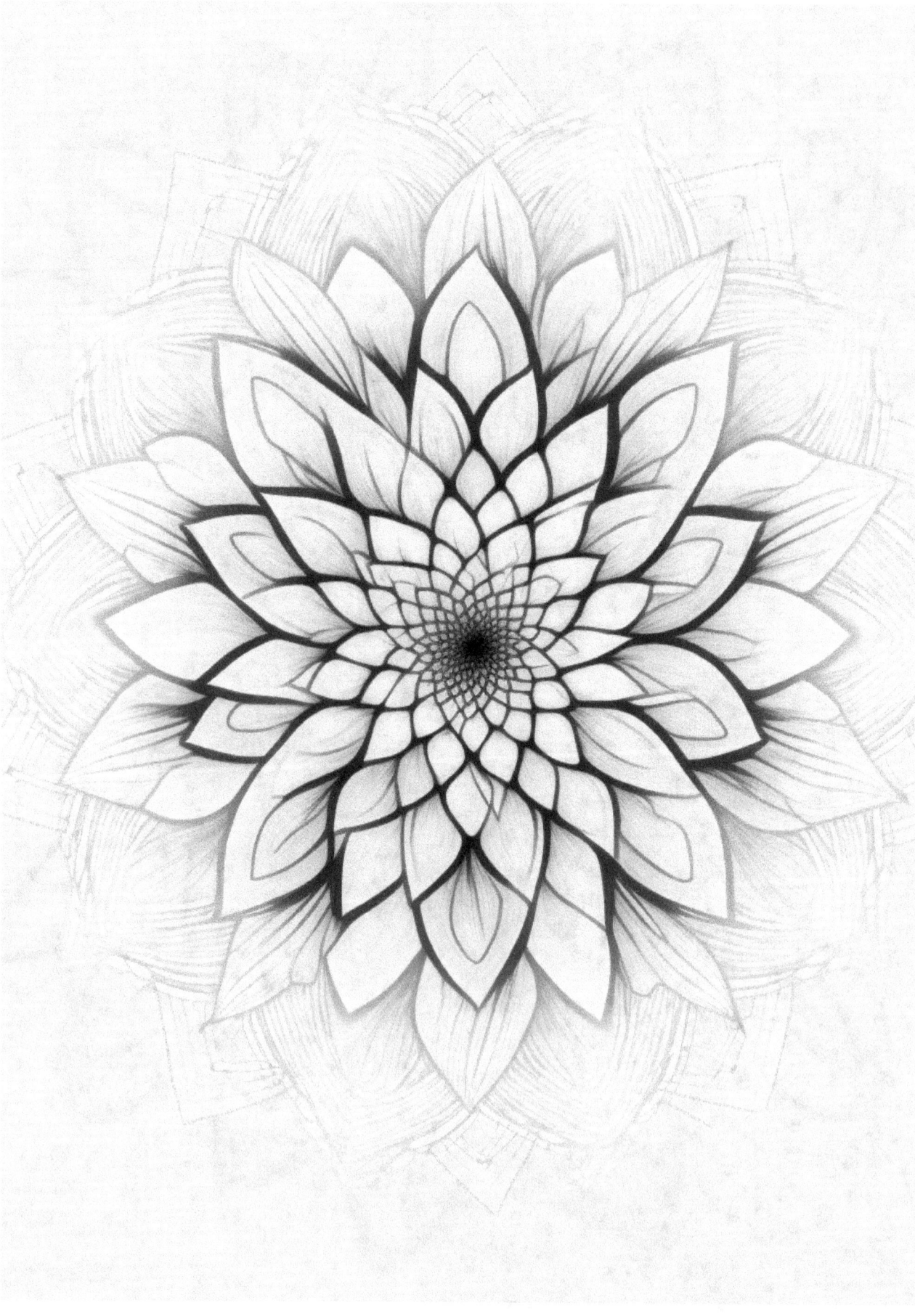

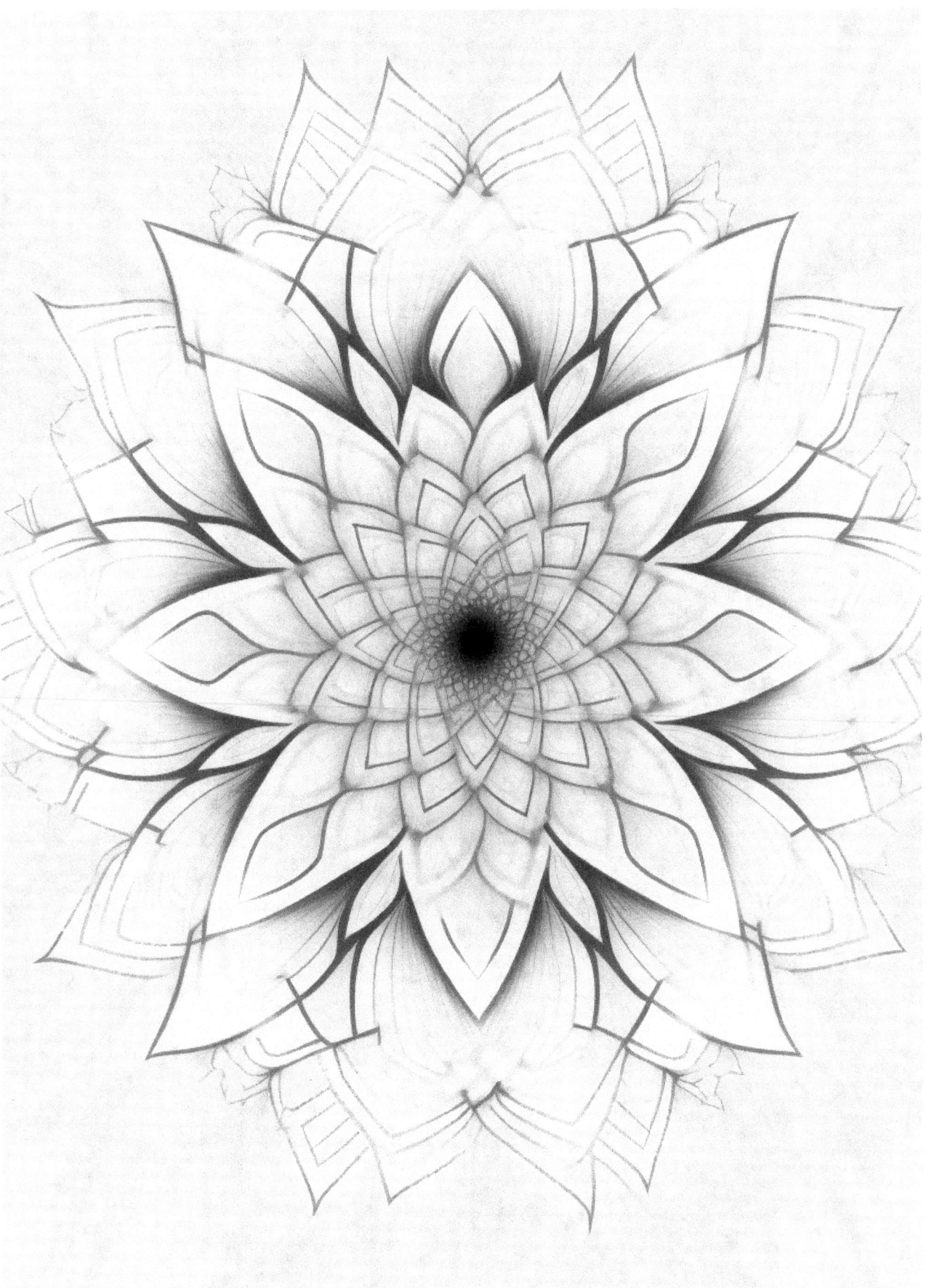

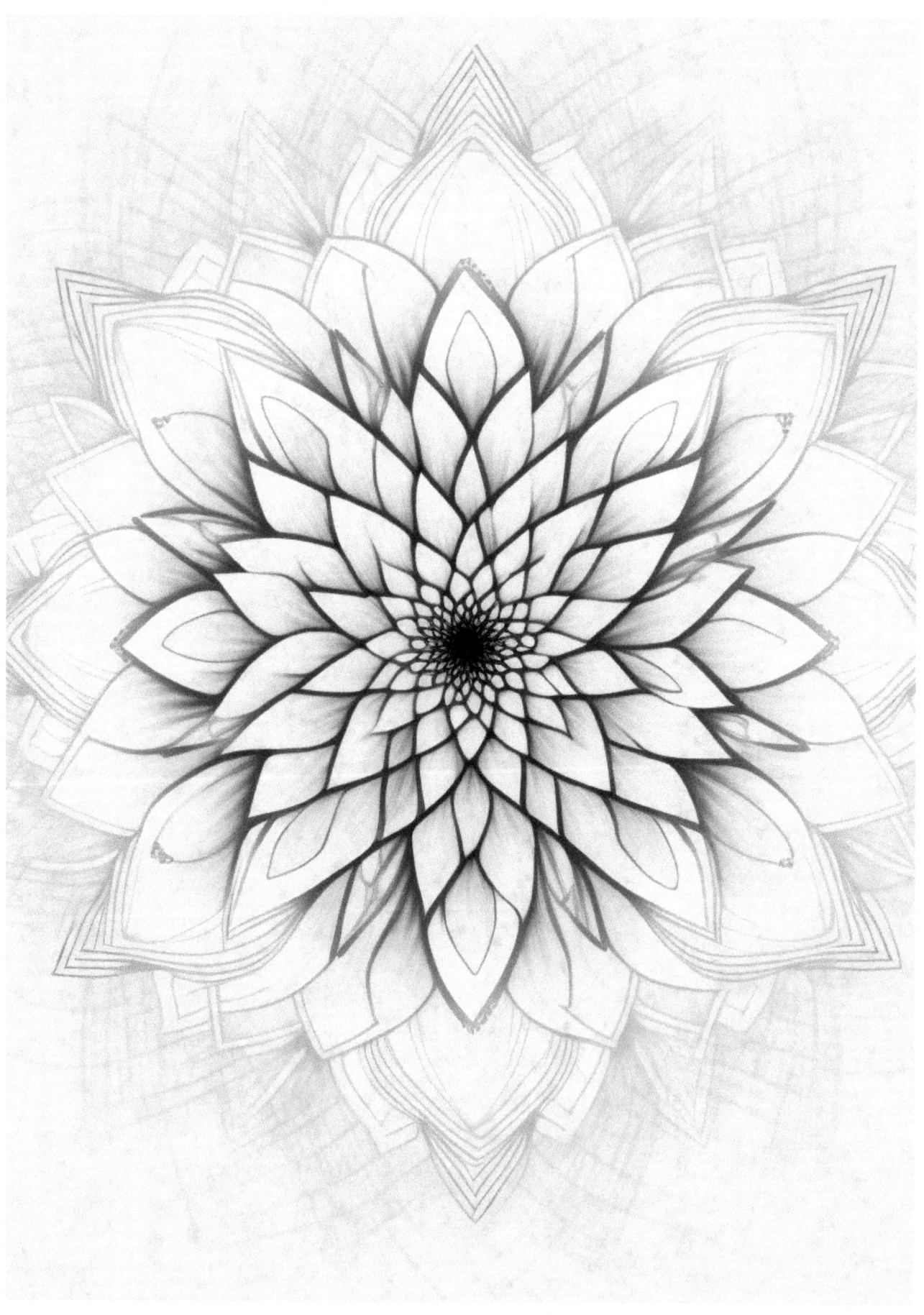

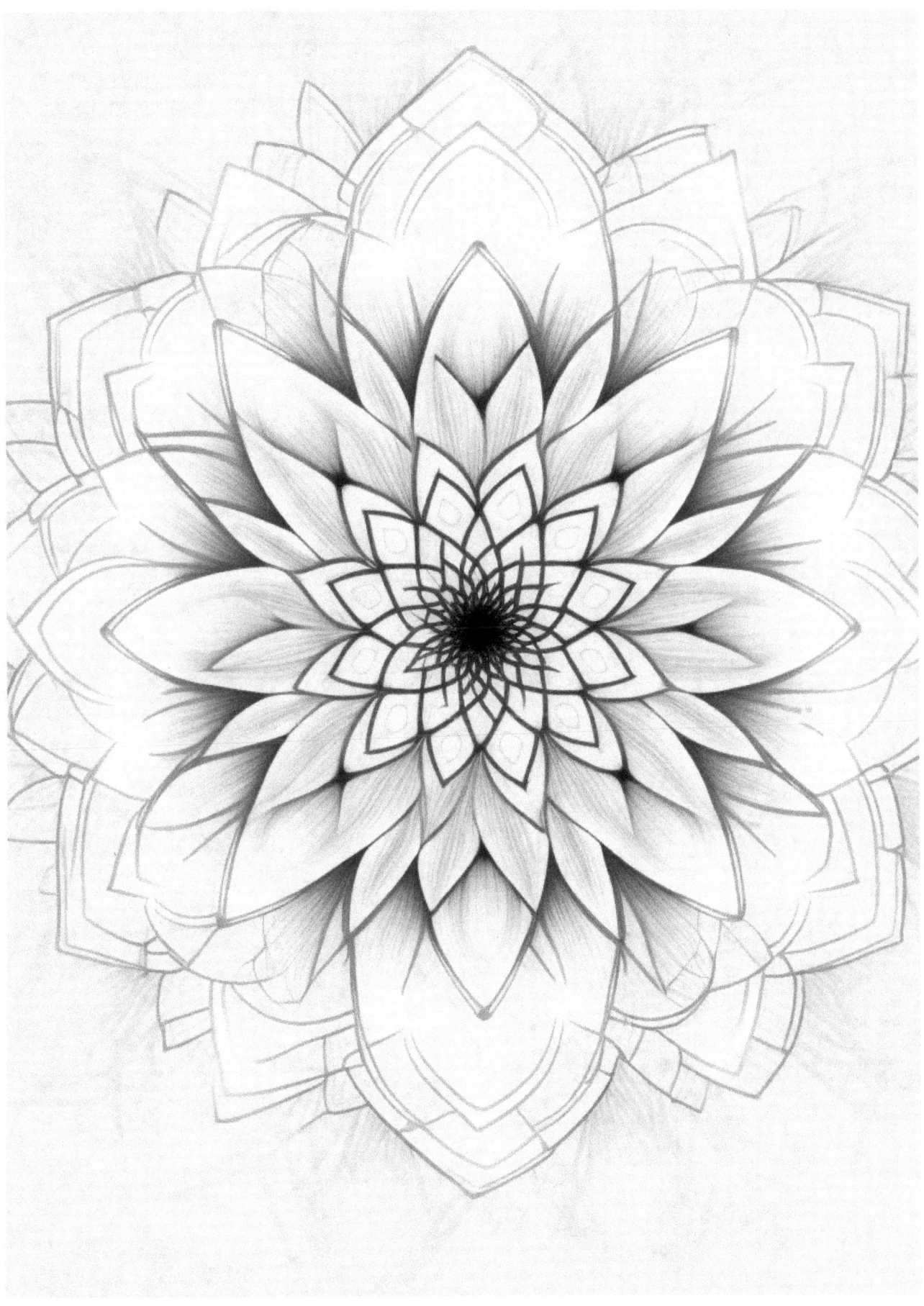